RELIGION
IN
THE AGE OF AQUARIUS

Books by John Charles Cooper

Published by The Westminster Press

Religion in the Age of Aquarius
The Turn Right
The New Mentality
Radical Christianity
and Its Sources
The Roots of the Radical Theology

RELIGION
IN
THE AGE OF AQUARIUS

BY
JOHN CHARLES COOPER

THE WESTMINSTER PRESS
PHILADELPHIA

ISBN 0-664-24905-1

LIBRARY OF CONGRESS CATALOG CARD NO. 77-133618

BOOK DESIGN BY
DOROTHY ALDEN SMITH

Published by The Westminster Press ⓐ
Philadelphia, Pennsylvania

PRINTED IN THE UNITED STATES OF AMERICA

For my children,
    in whom the Age of Aquarius
    is plainly evident in its goodness,

and for Roland Tapp,
    friend and teacher in the art
    of religious writing.

CONTENTS

ACKNOWLEDGMENTS

Acknowledgment is made to the following for permission to quote from their copyrighted publications:

Abingdon Press, *The Christian Agnostic,* by Leslie D. Weatherhead.

American Jewish Committee, "This Aquarian Age," by Milton Himmelfarb, *Commentary,* April, 1970. Copyright © 1970 by the American Jewish Committee.

George Braziller, Inc., *Witchcraft at Salem,* by Chadwick Hansen.

Communications, Research, Machines, Inc., "A Conversation with Harvey Cox and T. George Harris," *Psychology Today,* April, 1970, Vol. 3, No. 11. Copyright © Communications, Research, Machines, Inc.

Doubleday & Company, Inc., *The Other Side,* by James A. Pike with Diane Kennedy. © 1968 by New Focus Foundation.

Esquire, Inc., "Princess Leda's Castle in the Air," by Tom Burke, *Esquire,* Vol. LXXIII, No. 3 (March, 1970).

The Macmillan Company, *Science in the Modern World,* by Alfred North Whitehead, copyright 1925 by The Macmillan Company.

Sino-American Buddhist Association, passages from *Vajra Bodhi Sea,* April, 1970.

The Society for Comparative Philosophy, Inc., and Alan Watts, passages from *The Alan Watts Journal,* March, 1970.

United Church Press, "The Coming Dawn," by Esther Harding, *Quadrant 2,* Fall, 1968; "C. G. Jung and the Problems of Our Time," by Marie Louise von Franz, *Quadrant 5,* Fall, 1969.

The University of Chicago Magazine, "Four Searches for God in Man," by Samuel J. Beck, Vol. LXII, No. 5 (March/April, 1970).

The University of Chicago Press and Charles Hartshorne, *Philosophers Speak of God,* by Charles Hartshorne and William L. Reese, copyright 1953 by The University of Chicago.

WHEN PHILOSOPHY
IS NOT A GUIDE FOR LIFE

I am often asked my opinion of astrology and horoscopes, by students, colleagues, and people in general who know me as a philosopher with a particular interest in popular religion. These questions came long before the idea struck my mind of doing a book on the current rise of the importance of astrology and other manifestations of the occult. Now that it is general knowledge among the members of my university community that I am pursuing such an investigation, the questions have multiplied. For what it's worth, here is my answer, a dialectical one of yes and no—"dialectical" being both positive and negative, without being, I hope, ambiguous.

My answer revolves around one simple (logically speaking) observation that concerns the need of men and women for a freely selected yet stable and widely accepted guide for their lives. Astrology, as I see it, functions both positively and negatively as such a guide. In the absence of other guides, astrology serves, probably, a useful, positive function as a structure-giving, limit-setting, potentiality-opening set of symbols. Negatively speaking, astrology probably does young people especially a disservice in that it provides its guidance and support at best on the basis of a traditional wisdom that does not admit of accuracy, and at worst always on the basis of a pseudo reality, a fantastic vision of the nature of the universe. What I am saying, in brief, is that astrology is not much of a guide for life, but it is better than nothing. If philosophy (and psychology and sociology) cannot be our guide for life, then the stars are better than the darkness.[1]

INTRODUCTION

In the months since I completed the research and writing of *The New Mentality* (in the fall of 1968), I have continued to keep an eye on the trends and directions of American youth culture, through university teaching, serving a university church, and much traveling to many campuses as a lecturer and consultant. If anything, the publication of *The New Mentality* has brought me more young informants on the customs and usages of that developing majority of our population which is under twenty-five.

I am not ashamed of ending the previous study of the new mentality with the suggestion that a form of mysticism would be the religion of the future for the youths of this generation. I offered, in that study, the figure of Christ as a fit nucleus around which the inchoate yet deeply felt mystical yearnings of modern young people might coalesce. Looking at the multifaceted spiritual interests of today's young people, I see many who have come to just such a Christ mysticism. These people go under the name of "Jesus freaks" in some places and of "white magicians" in others. But what I should have pointed out more clearly was the possibility that this

mystical yearning might go to the bizarre extreme of
occultism. That movement toward witchcraft, magic, astrology, and even black magic, is what is happening today
among many of those who are the bearers of the new
mentality.

Samuel J. Beck, in his article "Four Searches for God
in Man," tells us:

As to our youth, they are, in their search, in imbalance,
obviously dominated by their feelings. In their liberated
energy, too frequently undirected, they are manifesting
that release of the demonic which Nietzsche apotheosizes
and which lives in all of us. Their acting-out has evoked,
as force usually does, counterforce, the backlash being
shrewdly manipulated by opportunists on the political
scene.[1]

This is a keen observation. Our youths are dominated
by their feelings, and those feelings are largely out of
balance and largely undirected. The demonic, sensual,
elemental human feelings are very much on the scene
today, and so is the concomitant spiritual state that ac-
companies the demonic—anxiety and fear.

I would say that one of the most widespread characteristics of this generation is anxiety. Many things contrib-
ute to this general anxiety—the war in Indochina, the
draft, economic dislocations following upon recent federal fiscal policies, the lack of a true understanding of
youthful needs by churchmen, educators, and legislators,
as well as the usual stress of growing up. In this general
state of anxiety, the younger generation are not unlike
their parents. But too many parents have adopted the
policy that if they pretend the anxiety isn't there, it will
go away. Additionally, the older generation have gone

very far toward drug abuse by (legally) tranquilizing its anxiety away.

The response of today's youths, as we shall see in these pages, has been different, and yet very similar. Young people haven't pretended that there is nothing to be "uptight" about, but they have turned to chemical release from their anxiety, just as their fathers and mothers did. Most young people taking drugs today really learned about pills and the possibility of drug relief at home, not on the streets with their peers. A drug-oriented culture such as upper- and middle-class America was bound to end up with child addicts sooner or later—and it has come very soon indeed.

Why speak of drugs? Because drugs and the occult occur together for the younger generation. They are two sides of the same coin called anxiety—anxiety that leads to alienation—over the state of the world today. And both drugs and the occult occur, for youths, in the general context of the religious dimension of life. Over and over, the young people who are participating in occult practices that come to my attention are found to be using drugs and are "on the outs" with their parents and their church.

One young lady with some profound personal problems finds herself drawn to occultism. Her anxiety over who she is has expressed itself in a very casual life-style that has widened the breach between herself and her parents. She is presently anxious over a curse or hex she fears has been laid on her. Recently she felt that a former boyfriend, killed a year before in an auto crash, was haunting her. When she tried to find solace with her parents, she was called a hippie, and her problems were dismissed. Again we see this pattern, a sense of alienation

provoked by the inability of the family and social institutions to deal directly and humanely with the problems
of young people. This alienation produces anxiety and
restlessness, and many times is expressed in hostility and
bizarre behavior.

Yet through the anxiety and loneliness of youthful
problems, the majority of young people continue to
search for meaning. Rejecting the traditional resources
of the church (as they feel the church has already rejected them), many youths turn to groups of their peers
who organize themselves around drug abuse and, increasingly, around occult practices. One of these practices is
the spontaneous séance held in the dormitory. One such
séance was described by three students in this way:

Just before Christmas vacation in 1969 ten girls gathered on the fourth floor of their dormitory, equipped
with two candles, a ouija board, and a sense of adventure,
to explore the spirit world. The room was darkened, the
ouija board was laid on their knees, and each one put an
index finger on the message indicator. Gradually the girls
began to realize that the questions were being communi-
cated through one of their number and the answers were
being spelled out by the ouija through spirits connected
with this girl's background. Nine of the ten girls were
absolutely convinced that a spirit was present and communicating with them. Now, months after the event, they
are still convinced of the reality of spirits and that spirits
spoke to them through the ouija.

This particular séance lasted from about 10 P.M. to
4 A.M. with a short break about 12:30. The spirits identified themselves as ancestors of some of the girls present
and mentioned wars and dates that could be checked.
One spirit identified itself as having lived in Bulgaria

and another as being French. Both of these spirits claimed to have died violent deaths. The Bulgarian spirit claimed to have been hanged by the French spirit as a result of a crime connected with a lovers' quarrel. The spirits came and went at intervals of ten to fifteen minutes and disappeared whenever the door was opened. Each time the spirit would leave and return, the candles would flicker, and the girl holding the candle testifies that the candle actually went out on these occasions and rekindled itself when the spirit returned. She is sure that no one was blowing out the candle.

At another point in the séance, the girls noticed a fishnet hanging in the corners moving when there was no wind and the heat in the room had been turned off. Several other spirits also made their presence known, including the Frenchman's wife, a spirit from Russia, and one from Hungary.

After the séance was over, they looked through the windows toward the cemetery located near the campus and all claimed that five of the gravestones were lighted up. The girls claimed that other girls along the whole floor of the residence looked out and saw this phenomenon and that even those who did not believe in such things had to admit that it was happening. Later they investigated the cemetery and found that one of the gravestones had a name that was a combination of two of the names given them by the spirits. The girls have continually checked the cemetery and found that the stones are not often lighted up but that it does happen occasionally.

These pages are written in the presence of the witnesses to the events described. They are not made up, and they did take place on the campus of a large university. The girls come from more or less usual church backgrounds and are not normally drug users; in fact, a large percentage of them do not use drugs at all. All claim that no one was high on drugs or alcohol at the time these events took place. All of them, with the exception of one firm non-believer, are convinced of the reality of spirits. Even the nonbeliever was upset by this experience and felt that something had happened. The girls have held other séances since that time and have become convinced that such experiences buttress their faith in God and that the motivation of the spirits is love. Additionally, they follow astrology, believe there is something to that, and have strong tendencies to believe that there may be witches and real powers of evil in the world. They also report up to seven or eight instances of levitation, in which one person is raised toward the ceiling by the mere touch of the index fingers of a half dozen people.

When asked why they explore these avenues of the occult, some answer that they have not found a help for their needs in the organized church. They stress the need for personal experience, which they seem to have found in such things as a séance. One girl is convinced that the spirit world is more important than the world we are living in. These experiences have confirmed her in her rejection of organized religion on the one side and in her belief in God on the other. For her, the meaning of life lies on the other side of death. She is almost unconcerned with politics and the ordinary course of affairs. Her experiences with the occult have made her religious, but in the otherworldly sense in which we think of the religion of the Middle Ages as being divorced from life.

The experience of the people described here is not surprising or unusual. There are thousands of young people like them, and the kind of magic or occultism in which they are engaged is white; that is, they are not dealing with the Devil, nor are they hostile to anyone. To the contrary, they are wholesome young people who retain a good deal of their Christianity and seem concerned to be moral and loving in their dealings with others. It is not with such as these that we should overly concern ourselves at this point; rather, it is with those young people who express, through their dabbling in the occult, not only their alienation from home and church but also their hostility against society and the older generation. In the following pages we shall be examining some of these more alienated and hostile groups. Then we will be able to see some of the demonic and destructive forces that are operating in our country because of the failure of organized religion, so far, to meet the needs of human beings in the Age of Aquarius.

J. C. C.

Eastern Kentucky University
Richmond, Kentucky

Chapter I

THE OCCULT
IN AMERICA TODAY

The scene is the emergency room of a large hospital in the western United States. A screaming, cursing young woman is brought in, wrists bleeding from an attempt with a knife upon her drug-dulled life. Battling both police and interns, the bleeding girl seems beyond medical help although several physicians stand back against the far wall. Suddenly the girl's eyes fasten on the face of a frightened young physician, fixing his attention by the intensity of her stare. "You can help me, man, you with the understanding face," she says in her first clear statement. Timidly the doctor approaches her and is allowed to bind her wrists. She whispers to him as he works: "I knew I could trust you. You're an Aquarius, aren't you?" Baffled, the doctor says he doesn't know. "Check on it, you're Aquarius; I know," the girl tells him. Later, troubled by the incident, the young doctor checks his birth date and his sun sign. He is an Aquarius.

Fiction? Not at all, but fact in the new America that is rising up out of the disappointments, failures, and compromises of the past decade. This event happened to my personal physician, a man who is not only my medical adviser but my friend. Just as have many other college professors, psychologists, and religious thinkers whom I know, my doctor and I agree that we heve entered the Age of Aquarius.

Youth's Appropriation of the Perennial Appeal of Astrology

My life has been bound up with young people professionally as well as personally for over ten years. Recently I have become more aware than ever before of the pervasive influence of the occult on the lives of my students. Of course, girls of sixteen to sixty have consulted their horoscopes occasionally since the beginning of civilization. When I was a college student, it was a great lark to go to the fair and have your palm read. But I cannot recall ever before the seriousness with which young people are taking the movement of the planets and the practices of sorcerers and seers. Sometime ago I polled my sophomore-level classes and asked them to tell me frankly whether or not they had more than a passing interest in the occult. Almost one half replied that they were at least interested in astrology and more or less believed there was something to it. I wasn't surprised that a lot of them were interested, but the percentage did surprise me. Long before I asked this group of students, I had read about and observed the ever-increasing influence of the occult on our daily life.

Without doubt, there is a strong symbolism of astrology in all the various movements, right and left, positive and negative, that are sweeping across the American landscape. To speak in Biblical language, ours is an apocalyptic age. This is a period in history when not only poets but politicians, theologians, and political scientists speak of the birth of one age and the death of another. We are living through an era when the young speak of the death of democracy in our country, ministers speak of the death of God from their pulpits, and ethical writers speak of the death of sex. Nothing seems to happen by degrees, nothing mild seems to be good or bad about our country, our civilization, or Christianity. Everything is painted in the most glaring colors and one comes to feel that great forces are at work building and destroying, perhaps without regard to our own wishes, even as the ancients might have considered the events of their history as due to the influence of the stars.

All that is needed is a pair of eyes to see and a radio to hear to learn of the influence of the occult on the young. Many songs clearly call for the Age of Aquarius to come; much of our young people's dress is decorated with the symbols of astrology and magic. At the same time that these young people may be rejecting the church with its symbols of the afterlife, the supernatural is coming back into their lives with a flood of reports of lives lived before this present one.

If it were only the very young who were involved, we might think the phenomenon of occult signs and symbols to be a passing fad, but it is obviously not only the young who are concerned. People of all ages seem drawn to astrology. For example, John Wanamaker's, a department store in Philadelphia, offers a computerized horoscope to anyone with $20 plus sales tax.[1] I think most of the people using this service are probably adult and well-to-do. It is clear also from the reports of the influence of astrologers such as Carroll Righter that their clients tend to be professional and well-to-do people. The current interest in the occult certainly cannot be labeled as only a youth

fad. Indeed, a number of universities sensitive to the interests of the public are offering credit courses covering
this aspect of life. I have lectured in such a course at a
large university.

The influence of astrology has even entered the crime
scene with the appearance of Dick Tracy's struggle with
Scorpio on the comic page and with the real-life tragedy
of the killer "Zodiac" who has terrorized the San Francisco area. By whatever means we use to measure things
—be it television, where the *TV Guide* for October 4–10,
1969, tells us that astrologers are security blankets for
many TV personalities, or *Time* magazine, which ran a
cover story on astrology and the new cult of the occult on
March 21, 1969, or the stage, where the folk-rock play
Hair tells us that the Age of Aquarius is dawning—it
would seem that astrology and the occult are very much
"now" indeed.[2]

A Time for Everything Under the Sun

The writer of the book of Ecclesiastes observes that
there is a time to throw stones away and a time to gather
them together—a time to scatter and a time to gather.
The writer (some three millennia ago) went on to declare
that there is a time for everything and that everything
will have its time. In this insight, the preacher is borne
out by modern psychological and sociological experience.
Man, and the societies he makes, tends to show a rhythm
of belief and disbelief, activity and passivity. Everything
has its time, and there is a time for everything under
heaven in the history of man. But more, there are times
specifically and intentionally disposed to throw stones, to
tear down, to devalue, to debunk. We have lived through

such a period since World War I. Now that period is over. Now the life-style of the people participating in what I have named "the new mentality" [3] is one of gathering stones together. It is this style that leads to the common experience of outrage that motivates the political protester and the peace demonstrator. Significantly, none of the protests or demonstrations is entirely free of some symbols and phrases taken from astrology or some other area of the occult.

Getting It Together

The most honorable compliment this generation can give anyone or anything is that he, she, or it is "together." This generation has seen the truth expressed by the poet:

> Things fall apart,
> The center cannot hold. . . .[4]

And it wishes to find again, to make anew, a center to hold the universe together. It is this desire to gather things together, to make sense out of the universe, which is the fundamental reason for the attraction of the younger generation to astrology and the occult. Our young, well-educated people are attracted by the promise of the occult to be an arcane science: a synoptic and synthetic vision of the wholeness of Being. Distracted by the scattering motions of the many individual sciences and learned disciplines, cheated out of a synthetic vision by a philosophy that tears language apart rather than putting Being together, offended by a religion that separates not only faith and reason but many times faith and action, the younger generation turns to astrology or to one of the

Eastern cults, out of a sense of despair. The rational and moral systems of the West, they feel, have failed them; now they seek vision in the dark side of Western thought or in the other-colored light that falls on them from the East.

This era is a seller's market for anyone who comes with a vision—no matter how myopic—of how the universe hangs together around the groping individual. It should occasion no wonder that many salesmen of the synoptic vision have arisen in our time. After all, many of these salesmen were always there. The occult tradition has existed as a contrapuntal element in Western thought from the beginnings of Western philosophy. Like the coals of a fire, occultism merely needed a freshened breeze to burst once more into flames. The breeze is blowing now, and it may become a hurricane. Right now, interest in the occult is the hottest thing in religion and popular philosophy.

The Significance of the Occult for the Youth Generation

The last several decades have revealed just how far modern science and twentieth-century experience have carried us beyond the place where human beings were profoundly aided by the symbols of Christianity. For a long time, indeed from the time of the Renaissance, thinking men were aware of the fact that the traditional symbols of the Bible and Christian history were being surpassed by human development. The entire history of modern theology has been an attempt to update these symbols and give them new power. In a strong sense, the revival of interest in astrology and the occult is an attempt to find a substitute set of symbols that convey the deepest feelings, hopes, and fears of human life, since the people drawn to them have found traditional religion wanting. The young person who consults his horoscope and that of the person he dates is looking for a norm, a guide of life, because either his traditional religious background has not provided such a norm or else its norm was so restrictive that it has been rejected. In a strange sort of way, the theologian can see that it has been precisely the attempts of modern theology to demythologize Christianity that have made it relatively ineffective as a satisfying system of spiritual guidance. Now that most theologians have stopped talking about the so-called three-storied universe of the Bible with its view of the world as located between heaven and hell, surprisingly the young are turning again to a supernatural vision of the universe as taught by astrology.

I have tried above to understand the current interest in the occult as a normal, or healthy, desire to find a religious framework for one's life. But there is another side to interest in the occult that is a less healthy and more psychotic phenomenon, an unhealthy tendency that occultism shares with traditional religion. This is the ever-present pull of superstition. Superstition grows out of anxiety; ultimately, its psychic power is derived from fear. Insofar as the conditions and structures of modern life are conducive to a life of anxiety, the conditions are right to foster superstitions.

Anxieties of a rational order, i.e., anxieties that represent a genuine responsiveness to actual problems in the external world, are stimulated chiefly by the sense (or state of awareness) that we are in the control of persons, ideas, ideals, values, powers, processes, and/or things and not in control of our own destinies. To the degree that man comes to see himself as a pawn in the vast games of

Realpolitik, business enterprise, and war (or cold war)—or, like the helpless passenger on an airplane, feels completely dependent upon the pilot and machine (and a vast organization) for his safety—to that degree the conditions for superstition are ripe. Soldiers in battle carry good-luck charms; soldiers in barracks generally do not. Increase the uncertainties of human existence, and the superstition factor increases proportionately. Seen in this light, the current popularity of astrology follows directly from an increase in anxiety among the population.

For whatever reasons the scholars may finally determine, interest in the occult, particularly in astrology, is stronger today than it has been in centuries. We need only look about us to see the hundreds of astrology books on the newsstands, the Devil fathering a child in a kind of reverse Christmas in the movie *Rosemary's Baby,* an Episcopal bishop (now deceased) who was convinced that he had spoken to his dead son through a medium,[5] and thousands of people in California uptight over hippie predictions that California will soon be swept away by earthquakes and tidal waves. Whether it is because of the age of anxiety we are living through, or because institutional religion has finally been revealed as void of the insight and symbols needed to help us make sense of ourselves, or for reasons not yet seen, we are definitely living in an Age of Aquarius, although we do not yet have the peace and love that youthful believers tell us Aquarius will bring.

The Philosophical Meaning of the Rise of Interest in the Occult

Whether it may mean a revitalized religious sense, or an expression of an inward, deeply traumatic sense of meaninglessness and lostness, or only a craving for bizarre novelties, the current rise of interest in the occult must be seen epistemologically (i.e., from the standpoint of our theory of how knowledge is gained) as a revolt against the scientific and technological rulership of the human mind in the twentieth century.

The mind of the intellectual who was educated some decades ago fairly faints when it tries to fathom the world view held by those who seriously consult their horoscopes before each undertaking, and must completely blink out at a clear picture of the mind-set of someone who practices magic and actually believes in the reality of Satan. *What* is the *content* and *organization* of a mind that apparently can harmonize the use of electricity, jet planes, and I.B.M. machines, not to mention heart transplants and the fact of nuclear energy, with a belief in reincarnation and the power of dark curses and the protective power of crosses and "haint strings"?

Obviously, much of the content of the minds of those people who wear amulets and work spells is the same as that of the passionately rational scientist's mind. Because they inhabit a common world and very often were educated at the same schools, it would have to be so. But there is a subtle and important difference: the scientist, with a rationally oriented mind, accepts the positivistic world view that makes technology possible and that is in turn shaped by technology. The occultist rejects this passionate positivism even while sharing in the material benefits it has produced. The situation is one of basic epistemology, and its logic is not unlike the situation in economics. Many of these "different" people who reject positivistic thinking also reject the mixed capitalism of the North American and Western European economic order, some preaching economic anarchism or extreme communism even while living off the surplus of the present system.

In short, occultism is a kind of philosophic anti-establishmentarianism—a protest that, of course, needs to be made, but that does not need to be made in such an extreme, antirational manner. I think there is an unconscious rejection of the whole civilization that the positivistic "hard" and "soft" (social) sciences have built up in the past one hundred years in this swing toward the Age of Aquarius and an emphasis on sensuality.

I am, furthermore, under the impression that the basic philosophic and spiritual rejection of this world view is responsible for the antisocial and self-destructive behavior involved in the drug movement. Rather than drug use's being the basis for hostility and rejection of rationality, discipline, system, and law, the rejection of positivism is at the root of both occultism and drug-taking. Similarly, such a basic rejection is responsible for the trend toward unintelligibility in art, music, and literature. The plotless movie, the topicless painting, the crash of sound that is music, all stem from the root rejection of the orderly progress of economics, science, society, and the arts which the nineteenth century rather seriously believed in, and which triumphed in the technological revolutions of the twentieth century, until it devoured its own credibility at Hiroshima, at Auschwitz, and in the pollution of the earth with its noxious by-products.

The underground stream of irrationality was always present, to be sure. Always there, lying "ready to hand," [6] as Martin Heidegger would say, until that day when it could become the creative "other," the option, the needed way of salvation. But that underground pipe had produced no more than a small leak in the positivistic faucet until the decade of the 1960's. Now it is a loud and steady, although still thin, stream of water staining and grooving the lily-white sink of modern philosophy, psychology, and the other "soft" as well as "hard" sciences.

The Cult of Evil

The rise of recent interest in the occult has paralleled the emergence of the life-style that has been called hippie. Along with a rejection of the economic values and moral standards of "middle America," there have been two major streams of activity that have flowed together to form the hippie life-style: the lure of drugs and the experiences available under drug intoxication, and the attractiveness of "way out" symbols and practices taken from such sources as the American Indians, Buddhism, and magic and witchcraft. I do not believe it to be true, however, that the hippie style of life is attracted to the evil that is found in some forms of occultism. Most of the cultic usage of the hippies has been directed toward what they call white magic. The kinds of minds that have formed cults of Satan are not hippie minds, since they are very active and aggressive minds, rather than passive, retiring minds.

The cults of evil are found alongside hippie communities in the same way that sharks are found near schools of fish. The members of the cults of evil prey on the hippies and through perversion take individual hippies into their group, particularly young impressionable women. The openness of hippie-type girls to sexual experimentation makes them an easy target for members of the evil cult, since these cults are largely based on group experimentation. In almost every case, the factor around which the group is built is the use of extremely toxic drugs. In the same way, the cults of evil draw membership from young men attracted to the motorcycle groups, for the bikers are constitutionally given to physical violence, drug abuse, and unusual forms of sexuality. Drawing on the susceptibility of the hippie girl to drug intoxication and complete openness with her sex life, and the same characteristics of the male in the motorcycle gang, together with his aggressiveness, a psychotic individual with leadership ability is able to build up a group that is capable of anything in seeking real or imagined revenge against society.

The best-known such group leader is Charles M. Manson, reportedly the leader of the group in California that allegedly killed Sharon Tate and her companions. A terrible fact that must be faced is that Charles Manson's group is not alone, but merely the first such group to come to spectacular public attention. Indeed, the Manson group in California is reported to have been responsible for a second killing very shortly after the first. The terrifying insight that we gain is that there could be many more such groups formed and outrages committed before we are able to cope with the needs and sicknesses of the minds that commit such acts. The revelation of the many cults of evil in California described in *Esquire,* March, 1970, and in such books as *The Killing of Sharon Tate,* by Lawrence Schiller, shows us that there are, indeed, hundreds of people for whom the worship of Satan, taken either seriously or symbolically as a mark of their alienation, is very real.[7]

The idea that American youth culture (and the political protest of the young) today exhibits a real struggle between the followers of Jesus and white magic on the one hand and the followers of Satan and black magic on the other probably seems absurd to anyone not in touch with young people. But it is an accurate reflection of what one finds if one takes the trouble to talk to young people (and some older people) and listens to the popular music of our day. The right-wing and left-wing extremes in politics, which I investigated in *The Turn Right*,[8] have their parallels in the struggles between Jesus people and Satan people in the occult underground.

Why the Occult Has Arisen in Our Time

When we examine the social world of young people in America in the 1970's, we find that instead of the falling away from religion that has often been predicted there is a religious ferment of vast proportions seething on America's college campuses, on the beaches and at other resorts where youth repair for leisure, and in the lives of young people already in the labor force. All across the country, as commentators on the right never tire of telling us, there is a great upheaval in the social situation. But whether one understands the trends toward dropping out of school, protesting Government policies, experimenting with drugs and sex, as being destructive and alienated or as being signs of a search for new meaning and for a new style of life, one cannot miss the fact that this is a period of spiritual creativity without parallel in recent times.

One might see the hot existentialism of the activists involved in social issues as well as the cold existentialism of the passive hippie type as two different ways of searching for salvation. The lure of Zen Buddhism and other mystic groups may be seen as a continuing effort by many people to find peace of mind, a state of being that this generation would call a "natural high." Such peace of mind for the individual self is a necessity for mental health in a world of mass conflict. The message of the Zen teachers, and other religiously oriented groups, seems to be that the peace that passes all understanding cannot be achieved by chemical means.[9]

The rise of interest in and belief in witchcraft may also be seen as part of the general religious ferment. Witchcraft may be arising because the quest for a new liturgy in the folk mass or in the "high" practices of the liturgical movement has failed to satisfy the modern psyche. Witchcraft is, after all, a series of rituals. These rituals may well be an attempt to recover the sense of the holy (in white magic) in our daily lives.

Finally, the mass religious phenomena of America in the '70s show us the ongoing search for community: community and peace for black and white, red and white, yellow and white. The peace movement and the various end-the-war movements that continue to attract the young may all be seen as quests for community, both domestically and internationally. In the words of Alfred North Whitehead concerning religion, we see something of the reason for the irruption of the occult in the last half of the twentieth century:

Religion is the vision of something which stands beyond, behind and within, the passing flux of immediate things; something which is real, and yet waiting to be realized; something which is a remote possibility, and yet the greatest of present facts; something that gives meaning to all that passes, and yet eludes apprehension; something whose possession is the final good, and yet is beyond all reach; something which is the ultimate ideal, and the hopeless quest.[10]

Yet, there are other reasons why the occult has returned and the Age of Aquarius has dawned.

The ageless appeal of astrology and other forms of occultism has been sharpened, reinforced, and generally enhanced by the emotional sterility of our industrialized, technologized civilization. Despite the appeal to man's sense of adventure in the great race for space and the dream of exploration of the planets, our civilization has largely wrung out the hardship, the challenge, the adventure of life, for many millions. Only war and the threat of war, only the appeal to fear and the appeal to the desire for security that prompts the arms race, makes any psychic "color" in the daily lives of most citizens. In the boredom and colorlessness of our daily lives there seems to be only a choice between apathy and violence, between living death and terror. Many now have gone beyond this choice to the options of violence and magic. By the same token, religion may be seen as *Weltanschauung,* or world view. The faith and love of the believer make up a perspective on life, a way of responding to other men and the events of the world.

Julio Caro Baroja, writing in *The World of the Witches,*[11] tells us that the essence of witchcraft lies in its view of reality, in other words, in its "blik." This perspective determines what the believer in witchcraft believes to be real and to exist. Baroja says that witchcraft is basically a notion that existed in times past almost everywhere and that still exists in some places, such as the Basque region of Spain and France, in the minds of people untouched by scientific thought. One wonders if this group

of believers in the occult might not now be growing because of an accession of disciples from more highly educated areas who have rejected the conception of reality
put forward by scientific thought.

Baroja offers us the further interesting insight that
witches (and believers in witches) tend to be much the
same whenever and wherever they happen to be. More-
over, the world situation in which witches and their believers are found tends to show definite social characteristics, whether we examine ancient or modern times. Perhaps we ought to ask the central and essential question:
What is the nature of reality in a world where there are
witches? The answer should prove enlightening when we
recall that the movement toward the occult has begun in
earnest only recently. *The historical circumstances of the
communities that believe in witchcraft are situations of
pestilence, war, and other disasters.*[12]

The anthropologist Malinowski echoes Baroja's insight.
Malinowski's thesis is that belief in magic is an answer
to the sense of despair that men and women feel in a
world that is beyond their control. Dr. Erland Ing, psychologist at the Veterans Administration Regional Hospital at Lexington, Kentucky, gives support to this thesis
with his report to the author that young veteran patients
with severe disturbances in their psychic lives sometimes
present him with their horoscopes so that he can "better
understand them." Lift the cover of belief in the occult,
and human anxiety excited by the movements of social
forces beyond individual control will stare you in the
face. The increasingly evident failure of Western traditional religious institutions to meet the psychic and social needs of Western men has sparked the emergence of
the occult in our day.

Dealing with the Occult with Faith and Love

Perhaps the best way of dealing with the rise of interest in astrology and the occult is to understand the youth among whom it has won most of its followers. In looking back over American history in the twentieth century, we find that the development of a youth culture is a unique and unusual thing not only in America but in the world at large. When we speak of "youth," we are speaking about a period in life roughly between the ages of fourteen and thirty years of age. We may observe that this new category of life is something of an invention of the twentieth century, based on the requirements and the opportunities of an industrial society. In prior eras there could be no "youth culture," since "youths" were not seen as constituting a separate category but as relatively inexperienced adults. These young adults were quickly drawn into the labor force or the army, or retained on the farm. It seems that all young people worked in the nineteenth century, and boys of twelve were not uncommon as drummer boys in the armies during the American Civil War.

Childhood itself may well be seen as a development of the increasingly industrialized and disciplined society of the second half of the nineteenth century. Despite growing feelings and laws against child labor throughout the nineteenth and into the twentieth century, child labor persisted in America until World War I in some areas. Before the coming of governmental regulations and the highly sophisticated machinery of modern technology, children were seen by adults and probably saw themselves only as miniature adults. Only in comparatively recent times, then, has childhood become a social institution.[13]

Looking further at the new phenomenon of a youth culture, we may observe that probably only in Western society since World War II has a cultural institution that includes fully grown persons called youths become possible. The reasons for such a development include the need for young persons to stay in school longer, indeed through college if possible, and also the increasing mechanization of industry, which has created less need for a large labor force. The fact that industry did not need everyone right away and that education was becoming more and more important made conditions right to create another social group. Being creative and energetic, this bloc has by now largely imposed its fashions of dress on the older groups of people as well as on the younger ones and seems now in process of imposing its moral values on the older generation. Out of the example of spontaneous sex and experimental attitudes toward sex among members of the youth group has come the impetus among the age group over thirty to experiment with group sex, wife-swapping, and other sociological oddities.

For some vague sociological reason, there is a law of social behavior that works roughly like this: younger people tend to imitate the people who are ahead of them in school—a year or two older—and this imitation cycle holds true from kindergarten through grade school, through high school to college and university to graduate school. But the cycle of imitation stops roughly at the end of the educational process. College, university, and graduate school students, for the most part, do not imitate "adults," or the generation older than themselves. Some students do so, of course, but these conforming students generally seem to be socially backward in some respect, from rural and depressed areas, enrolled at marginally ranked smaller colleges and state universities, or in some other respect out of the mainstream of youth culture. For most college students, it is a case of being imitated by high school students (who are imitated by junior highs, etc.) but not of imitating the older generation. The creative, imaginative, initiative-taking period seems to lie somewhere in the high school and college years, and it is these people who most clearly reflect the life-style and world view I call the new mentality.

The most interesting aspect of the imitation of college students by younger people is that adults beyond the college years also imitate the college generation, in dress, speech, and morals. One sometimes wonders what, if anything, the generation gap is.[14]

The Age of Aquarius

The Age of Aquarius is now an internationally known and used tag for our historical period. One cannot turn on the television or radio without hearing something that refers to the Age of Aquarius. Perhaps we ought to define what we mean by using the phrase. The term "Age of Aquarius" is commonly used by astrologers, by youth in general, and by the public at large to denote the present era of history, which is declared to be one in which world peace and brotherhood will come. The world, according to professional astrologers, has just entered the Aquarian Age. Such an astrological age is calculated on the basis of the movement of the vernal equinox westward across the heavens. This equinox moves about fifty seconds per year, and this movement over a period of some two thousand years has brought the point of equinox from within the imaginary boundaries of the zodiac's sign called Pisces into the sign called Aquarius. According to the cosmological astrologers, the Age of Aquarius, since it is under a light, airy sign, will be a period when mankind will be filled with aspirations and will move toward hope and faith. In contrast, the Age of Pisces, a watery sign, was characterized by skepticism and disillusionment. According to Carroll Righter, a very well known astrologer, the Age of Pisces was an age of cares and sorrows, whose determining point was the death of Christ. By Righter's calculations, the world entered the Age of Aquarius in 1904, and this age will be one of joy and accomplishment centered on the life of Christ.

I think it is important that we note that the astrologers who teach the coming of the Age of Aquarius and the young people and others who glory in its coming are realistic enough to recognize that the Age of Aquarius is an age of coming peace. Peace and harmony are potential, not actual, coming by a promise, not by a guarantee. Indeed, the conception of a coming age of peace is itself the mark of a vital hope and faith, for there are not that many signs in the world that such an era is dawning. And Aquarius is a time of joy, for if one has a thing he can lose it, but if he has something only by promise it cannot be lost but can be fully enjoyed by anticipation.

Apparently, astrology has provided more meaningful symbols for the expression of the innermost desires and hopes of the current younger generation than has traditional religion and politics. One would think that astrology would have a tremendous credibility gap when addressing young people who belong to the television generation and who are by everyone's measurement the best educated generation in American history. However, the turn toward the occult is not a rational movement at all but may actually be a movement of great interest and attraction simply because it goes against the rationality of this century. Perhaps, in the words of a popular song, youthful practicers of the occult say, "If I can't arouse heaven, I'll raise hell." In this respect, as I have observed above, the tendency to embrace the occult, like the trend to experiment with drugs, is a mark of youth's alienation and its rejection of the positivistic science of our age. Amazingly, it is not astrology or even witchcraft that runs into a credibility gap with youth and with the alienated older allies of youth but, rather, Christianity and American politics.

The Getriebenen, *or the Driven Ones*[15]

The later years of the decade of the sixties and the opening of the decade of the seventies have been a period in which the widespread use of various drugs is a significant social phenomenon. The recourse of many youths to marijuana, LSD-25, and the many other drugs available through underground channels is a mark of the alienation and anxiety felt by large groups of high school and college young people. These youths may be called the *Getriebenen,* the Driven Ones. The ultimate alienation of their behavior may be the fusing together of the cult of drugs with the cult of sex in the "Satan" or black-magic groups to be discussed later in this book.

We will mention here only the following facts as part of our introduction to the rise of occult influences on our day: First, the experience of mind expansion or hallucination with its thought distortion and perception distortion produces in some minds internal experiences that may seem close to the fantasy world of magic and the supernatural. The person who has frequently experienced such changes in his state of consciousness may become more willing to accept and value the weird and "far out" symbols and practices of the occult. Secondly, the use of drugs and the practice of occultism both constitute their practitioners as "countercultures." The person involved in such a subculture begins to see himself and to be seen by others as an outsider. Ultimately, the nonmedically based approach of the several law enforcement agencies begins to cause the user of drugs to feel himself to be one of the *Vertriebenen*, the Expelled Ones.

Erik H. Erikson, in his *Insight and Responsibility*, helps us to understand that the feeling of being driven and even of being driven out is not necessarily pathological by reminding us that "there is a 'natural' period of up-rootedness in human life: adolescence." [16] It is no psychological accident that both drug abuse and the lure of the occult are strongest in their appeal to young people in the process of undergoing adolescence or early adulthood. Youth is, after all, concerned chiefly with self-discovery. Young people are egocentric, in the epistemological sense, which means that they see the world from their own perspective and give little attention to other people's points of view. Deeply concerned to discover who and what they are, they plumb the recesses of their inner being and uncover what all men who reflect upon themselves find—contradictions within themselves. Everyone of every generation remains such a bundle of interrelated contradictions, of course, but the adult has deadened his awareness of his inner contradictions while the youth has not.

In search of a way to live with his contradictions, the sensitive youth looks beyond the behavioristic materialism that underlies so much of modern education and advice and thus is open to the experiment with drugs or to recourse to the occult. When a young person has a problem so basic (the question as to who he is and what value and meaning his person has) that it makes other problems irrelevant, it should not surprise us to find that he is rather technological and manipulative (and not reflective and cautious) in dealing with either drug or occult phenomena. The driven young person (and all of us are "driven" to some extent) doesn't stop to ask, "What effect will this drug have on me tomorrow, next week, ten years from now?" Rather, he takes the drug and finds out what it does for him now. This is the experimental, trial-and-error method that Americans have gloried in for a long time—their scientific pragmatism. The youth who "drops" an "acid" (LSD-25) dose is "learning by doing" in the best progressive educational style. Since our norms and value systems have largely broken down in this country, one wonders what other basis for decision is really viable for any young person who is not brainwashed and dominated by adults.

The most demonic aspect of this whole drug experimentation wave is the harsh and absolutely unscientific use of police power and punitive sentences on youthful offenders against the drug laws. These statutes are based on the philosophy that drug use grows out of hedonism only. Such is not the case. Similarly, we may observe that the young seem to *practice* the occult in its various forms of astrology, palmistry, and witchcraft (to a lesser extent), whereas the older "believers" *believe* in what they practice. The question of "truth," particularly with reference to astrology, never comes up with youth, as far as I have been able to find in my investigations. As Harvey Cox has correctly noted:

Do you know what people are saying when they ask your sign? They are saying I want to relate to you, to be intimate with you in this kooky, interesting, groovy way—a way that is going to blow the minds of those god-damned rationalists. The logical people who have organized our society have defined us into categories that we can't live in.[17]

My research validates what Cox says, but while he stresses the anti-establishmentarianism of the resort to astrological "games," I would underscore the connection of the pragmatic use of horoscopes with the technological, manipulative approach to life that gives the Establishment its worldly power. Young people use the occult when it is *useful* and *drop it* when it is not. In their approach to the mystic arts, young Americans are not unlike liberal theologians who use whatever is useful in religion and drop the rest. Young people have told me over and over again: "Astrology works. We don't know how, and we don't care." This is an extremely technological, pragmatic attitude, for technology is concerned only with "how to use," not with "Why does this thing act this way?" Science, in the sense of research that aims for universal knowledge, theoretical constructs, asks "How?"; philosophy and religion traditionally have asked "Why?" Youths who "use" the occult today seem never to ask either "How?" or "Why?" but only "What?" How I become full of the personality traits of the Aries type, and why I should be an Aries type just because I was born on April 3, never enters the mind of the user of astrology. The question is, "What sign are you?" Perhaps this is the greatest strength and the ultimate weakness in the lure of the occult. Perhaps when the occult asks "How?" and "Why?" it begins the process that turns the mythological into science and philosophy.

Chapter II

COMICS, MOVIES, MEDIUMS, AND MURDER

Harvey Cox has observed:

The astrology trip is a form of play, of relating to each other in ways we don't have to take too seriously until we know we want to. In a broader sense, astrology and drugs and Zen are forms of play, of testing new perceptions of reality without being committed to their validity in advance—or ever.[1]

Cox is right, of course, but only on one level. What is wrong about this assessment is the mistaken view that play is somehow opposed to work, or that playfulness is the opposite of seriousness. This view is simply not true as a phenomenological description of either the social world or the human psyche. Indeed work is but a classification of play in the sense of role-playing. Most games are taken far more seriously by the game players than work is by workmen. The proof of this lies in the fact that we play at our work usually only for some *extrinsic* reward of status and money, while we play at a game for the *intrinsic* rewards of the game itself. Only theoretically, in a profession, does the intrinsic worth of the role-playing itself equal or surpass the extrinsic rewards of status and financial reward. In a work-compulsive society, Cox's apology for play is valid and needed, but the background of the puritan ethic in America distorts the true situation of man who, like the child he forever remains, plays at those things which interest him if he is fortunate, or at those things which are available, if he is not. As Cox demonstrates in his writings, his profession is his play, playing Harvey Cox, and this is a beautiful and serious thing.

Let us investigate the playfulness of the recent upsurge of interest in the occult and then go on to see its ultimate seriousness. The playfulness of the lure of the occult is seen in comics and movies as well as in the daily reference to the star charts. The seriousness of the effect of the rise of occultism today is seen in the prominence of mediums, the drift of clergy and lay people to spiritualism, and the appearance of the occult murder.

The Occult Seen as Playfulness

The young girl who asks a boy she has just met what his sign is is being playfully serious with him and also seriously playful! The boy who responds with the information is acting in the same manner. The emphasis here is, as Cox states, on relating to one another in a joyful, free way. There is also, however, a question that is silently asked: How serious can I get about you?

After two years of observing a number of college students (and some younger high school and junior high school students), I have come to realize that *the trend toward interest in astrology* is precipitated in the young person by a number of factors, which we have discussed above, including the drive to escape insecurity and anxiety, the need to discover norms and guidelines for one's life, and the expression of one's sense of alienation from the present society's goals and means of attaining those goals.

Harvey Cox may be far more perceptive than the rest of us when he declares that ours is a fact-oriented society and therefore:

Those who had a penchant for fantasy never really felt at home. They were driven out of religious institutions. . . . [And yet] today's rebirth of fantasy may be a deceptive flush on the cheek of a dying age.[2]

Cox goes on to say:

People all over the world are turning, often desperately, to the overlooked corners and freaks that were never completely systematized. . . . Also with the slippery stuff that never found a place in it: astrology, madness, witches, drugs, non-Western religions, palmistry and mysticism, shoddy or serious.[3]

People are turning now to the overlooked, the freaks, the "slippery stuff," and this turn toward the occult, visible in all Western societies, I have called the real, inner meaning of the phrase "the Age of Aquarius." We can trace this turning to the strange (and forbidden?) in the comic strips that form so large a part of our popular culture. Of course, the world of magic and the occult has never been entirely missing from the comic page—"Mandrake the Magician" has been a favorite strip of many for years. However, in 1969–1970, the two most conservative comic strips (from the standpoint of political philosophy), as well as two of the oldest, began series that reflected the current interest in astrology and the occult. In an exciting story, the "law and order" protagonist, Dick Tracy, battled Scorpio, an arch villain who kept his own private astrologer. Little Orphan Annie (in November, 1969) concerned herself with magic and Eastern priestly types, but with the typical conservative cynicism that is the invariable companion of Annie's lack of eyes!

In the cinema we have the phenomena of *Rosemary's Baby* (also popular as a book) and the tripartite foreign movie *Spirits of the Dead,* as well as a host of "campy" horror movies about witches, Satan cultists, Dracula, and Frankenstein, which play regularly to youth audiences at drive-in movies.

Rosemary's Baby was easily the hit of the year in which it appeared—at least for young people and the alienated of all ages. Yet, as William Hamilton remarks:

The theology of the film, in spite of the Marxism of Roman Polanski, is nearly orthodox: God is dead, and this is a horrible fact, and the demons will get you if you don't watch out. The nearest parallel in recent literature to the theology of this film is John Updike's *Couples* in which the author says all this hanky-panky is clearly inevitable since they're turning their backs on God.[4]

Rosemary's Baby is significant because it links up the "death of God" movement begun by Thomas J. J. Altizer and William Hamilton with the more recent emergence of what Hamilton calls "the occult underground." Indeed, at the end of the film, the witch-leader, Castavet, cries out in triumph:

God is dead! God is dead and Satan lives! The year is One, the first year of our Lord! The year is One, God is done![5]

Mediums, Messages, Memorials

Perhaps the most dramatic example of the surfacing of the occult underground into the mainstream of both church and academic life was the growing, and publicly recorded, fascination with and belief in the occult by the late Bishop James A. Pike. Not since the interest in psychic phenomena shown by Victorian- and Edwardian-era intellectuals has mediumship been quite so important and "respectable" in the English-speaking world. Bishop Pike has recorded his journey into the realm of the spiritualists in his interesting book *The Other Side*.[6] My interest in discussing Bishop Pike's book is simply to illuminate the influence of the occult on intellectuals in our day, and not to criticize the late bishop. This is a hard line to follow, for unfortunately Bishop Pike's encounter with the occult grew out of a great family tragedy, the suicide of his son. The book details with great patience the overcoming of the bishop's prejudices against the psychic area and his growing belief that his dead son was attempting to contact him "from the other side."

Bishop Pike, who recently died while on a journey in Israel's Dead Sea area, was nothing if not painfully open and frank. Reading *The Other Side*, no matter what one's opinions about the bishop's theology or psychic phenomena, is a moving, sometimes almost an unbearable, experience. The bishop clearly was skeptical, at first, of the reality of psychic phenomena, such as medium-transmitted messages from the dead or the moving of various items in a room.

Perhaps it is less important to review what Bishop Pike records in his book than it is simply to note its appearance and refer the reader to the book itself. Bishop Pike, it seems to me, never lost his objectivity as a theological thinker and as a trained lawyer in his investigation of what he reports really happened to him. He found it difficult to accept the view of the world that the existence of such psychic phenomena made necessary in contradistinction to our usual view. However, his final decision to accept the reality of messages from the other side he clearly states to rest on an intuition: "There remains an intuitive perception of personality which is impossible to dismiss when one is analyzing any such experience piece by piece. It is not difficult to forget it, and I often do, for it is an all-encompassing feeling rather than a set of facts or a series of statements. Nevertheless, the sense that one is communicating with persons is so strong as to be almost the most convincing single factor leading to the affirmation of communication with the deceased." [7]

This seems like a very sensible decision, one based on experience as well as intuition. It is, after all, the kind of intuition that underlies our acceptance of the fact that the person we are talking to on the telephone is actually the person we think it is and not an actor imitating that person's voice. The same kind of intuition underlies our acceptance of the fact that a letter is from the person it purports to be from. After all, with the typed letter we do not have handwriting to go on and we do not have the inflection of the voice or the opportunity to cross-question the person we are communicating with. We can only intuit the personality of the writer from our knowledge of what the writer is like. On this basis, we can only take Bishop Pike's word that his intuition was sound, or at least convincing enough for him to say in closing his book:

Until we have more understanding and better concepts and words to use to talk about the experience (and, for that matter, about the daily interpersonal relationships with which we are more accustomed), and in the light of all that has been said here, in response to the oft-asked questions—the ones the reader also no doubt has in mind—"Do you believe in ongoing personal life?" and "Do you believe you have been in touch with your son?" (since what is asked is not "Do you know . . . ," but "Do you believe . . ."), my answer is Yes, I do.[8]

On the negative side, I must say that one of the things that disturbed me personally about Bishop Pike's book was his reference to appearances of Paul Tillich in the context of psychic communication from the beyond. Paul Tillich was my teacher, and not only my teacher but the subject of my doctoral dissertation. Paul and Hannah Tillich were my good friends and Hannah still is. What troubles me is that I know Paul Tillich was scornful of such psychic communications while living. Once at a meeting in his living room, I asked him to explain what the symbol "eternal life" meant in his systematic theology. I got an ambiguous answer but one that seemed to use some traditional language. It satisfied me at the time, I must admit. However, it did not satisfy one of my fellow students, Clark Williamson, now professor at Christian Theological Seminary in Indianapolis, Indiana. Williamson said sharply to Tillich, "Are you implying some kind of survival of a spirit?" To this Tillich said, "I do not believe in ghosts." This was said in a rather deep and puckish voice, and was a phrase to be repeated several times in the remaining period that I knew Tillich. Therefore, I must say that Pike, who also knew Tillich, must have been aware of Tillich's feelings about the beyond.

Pike either felt the affirmation of his intuition of Tillich's personality to be so strong that he would go against Tillich's own opinions while alive, or else he simply didn't care.

Intellectual Interest in the Occult

Apparently, Western society has always had a small group of intellectuals who have dabbled in the occult and who have engaged in séances, spirit rapping, and other occult arts. We know of the interest of Sir Arthur Conan Doyle, the creator of Sherlock Holmes, as well as the interest of the outstanding philosopher and one of the founders of psychology, William James. However, up until the last few years this group of intellectuals had shrunk to a very small number. It would seem that what we are seeing now is not something new so much as something old experiencing a large new growth. Of course, there has always been, throughout the twentieth century, one intellectual stream that has given respectability to interest in the occult, and that is the movement in psychology founded by C. G. Jung. The C. G. Jung Foundation for Analytical Psychology, Inc., carries on in America the interest of Switzerland's Jungian Institute in the interpretation of dreams and the fantasies of mentally disturbed patients by way of recourse to the mythological tradition of the world, including the occult. Jung has said that he often found it helpful to have the horoscope of the patient cast when he was trying to treat the patient for some disturbance. Jung may be criticized for this by some psychologists, and yet he really is following the lead of Sigmund Freud, who first restored dreams to the catalog of items to be studied by the physician in his attempt to assist the patient.

The interpreters of dreams, such as the "old gypsy women" who flourished in the villages of Europe, had destroyed the status of the dream in the eyes of science until Freud very courageously chose the dream as a method to carry on his psychoanalysis. Actually Jung simply furthered this work and attempted to create a vast interlocking "map" of the myths of mankind, which seemed to him to recur again and again in the dreams of human beings from all over the world. Jung came to believe that the materials that make up myths, i.e., symbols, actually constitute a kind of racial memory that is inborn in a human being regardless of his time and place. These "archetypical images" are codetermining influences on human life along with the freely chosen actions of the human person. Jung spent his lifetime trying to devise a complete description of the myths and symbols that make up mankind's heritage.

It is from Jung that we receive great support for the view that man's symbol-making capacities are the qualities of his being that make him distinctly human. An example of an archetype would be the image of the original or cosmic man. This is the figure of Adam in the Bible, and of Adapa in ancient Babylonian mythology. This original man is regarded as the life principle, the inner meaning of man's life in history. We know that in the speculation of the Hebrew rabbis the figure of Adam came to be considered as a kind of symbol of the whole physical universe. In the sense that the Stoic philosophers considered the whole universe to be living and considered each man to be but a cell in the tremendous body of the universe, similarly the rabbis saw that each man was included in Adam. This archetype is very clearly seen in the New Testament, in the writings of Paul. Paul writes in Rom. 5:12-19:

Therefore as sin came into the world through one man and death through sin, and so death spread to all men because all men sinned—sin indeed was in the world before the law was given, but sin is not counted where there is no law. Yet death reigned from Adam to Moses, even over those whose sins were not like the transgression of Adam, who was a type of the one who was to come.

But the free gift is not like the trespass. For if many died through one man's trespass, much more have the grace of God and the free gift in the grace of that one man Jesus Christ abounded for many. And the free gift is not like the effect of that one man's sin. For the judgment following one trespass brought condemnation, but the free gift following many trespasses brings justification. If, because of one man's trespass, death reigned through that one man, much more will those who receive the abundance of grace and the free gift of righteousness reign in life through the one man Jesus Christ.

Then as one man's trespass led to condemnation for all men, so one man's act of righteousness leads to acquittal and life for all men. For as by one man's disobedience many were made sinners, so by one man's obedience many will be made righteous.

According to the orthodox theology of Christianity, following Paul, man is a sinner from birth because of Adam's sin. According to the occult tradition of Judaism (the Cabala), the souls of all human beings were contained in Adam, just as the wick of a lamp is made up of many threads. The early German myths (the Edda) saw the primal man as a giant, Ymir. Chinese mythology saw the original material of the universe as the giant P'an ku. The Indian Vedas tell us of Yama, the ancestor of all men. Persian mythology gives us the story of Gayomart, out of whose body all the matter of the universe was formed.

When we recall that the basic thrust of the younger generation is for each young person to discover who he is and to form a satisfactory concept of his identity, we can see why the images and symbols of the occult (so like the archetypes of the unconscious) appeal to them. We can also see why "getting it together" is the watchword of the hippie, or alienated, younger generation. The younger generation, and their intellectual leaders and sympathizers, are not so much in a stage of revolt as they are in a state of outrage over the shortcomings, the "loose ends," of Western society. We may see the hippie, occult movement as a phenomenon with two sides: one side a feeling of outrage at what previous adult generations have done to the world, and the other a highly idealistic desire to love and to be loved individually and collectively without regard to nation or race. Seen thus, the new mentality takes on its proper shape.

Marie Louise von Franz, writing in her article on "C. G. Jung and the Problems of Our Time," observes of the symbol of the primal man:

This decay of a gigantic man into the universe, or his transformation into it, describes, if we see it from a psychological standpoint, a most primordial preconscious act of projection, an event which leads to that state of affairs which anthropologists and psychologists describe as the most original state of mankind, and of the child, namely the state of a complete participation mystique with the whole surrounding world. Jung has called this state archaic identity. In it there is no ego consciousness, no discrimination between subject and object, or between ego and self. They are all one.[9]

Could anything be more descriptive of the inner aims and goals of the hippie movement and especially of those who are seeking some sort of social salvation through drugs and the occult?

The Dark Side of Interest in the Occult

We have already spoken of superstition as the inevitable accompaniment of taking the occult seriously. The drive to find unity through the occult, as healthy as that may be, seems invariably to involve fear, disfunctionality, and bizarre behavior. The wearing of "haint strings," or symbols designed to ward off evil fortune or bring good luck, by hippies and other college students today reminds one of the spitting and finger signs made by southern Italians to ward off the evil eye. It is said that the cinema director Fellini, for instance, made his part of the motion picture *Spirits of the Dead,* even though he didn't want to do so, after he received a certain reading of his horoscope. Occult-based superstition, we are told, even entered the Second World War when the British Secret Service assigned Ian Fleming (of James Bond fame) to take advantage of Hitler's belief in astrology. (It is known that Hitler kept an astrologer for consultation.)

In our own country today, we have the fusing of superstition and fact in the anxiety of thousands in Southern California who fear the destruction of the state by earthquake and flood. In this case superstition adds to reasonable anxiety only to a degree, since Southern California does have the dangerous San Andreas Fault, which could cause problems at any time. However, the predictions of imminent destruction by astrologers, hippie seers, and sectarian religious prophets have added to the fear of many. A novel was written entitled *The Late, Great State of California,*[10] and it proved quite successful. Apparently people are really interested in that which makes them fearful. The testing of atomic devices underground in the Aleutian Islands off Alaska was strenuously opposed by many Californians who feared that the shock waves from the atomic blasts might trigger the dreaded final earthquake in California. Opposition groups did not deter the Government; the tests were begun, and so far California has not sunk into the ocean.

The Revival of Satanism in Our Day

Actually, the concept of Satan, or as he is popularly called in English, "the Devil," is a very common religious idea. The concept of a personal power of evil probably originated in the dualistic religious philosophy of Persia, what we call Zoroastrianism. Zoroaster taught that there are two equally basic divine powers, the one good (Ahura Mazda, or Ormazd) and the other evil (Angra Mainyu, or Ahriman). Ahriman's name appropriately means "the hostile spirit." This basic model for the Devil is said to be coeval in origin with Ahura Mazda, the good spirit, but is not really eternal, since Ahriman is destined to be defeated and cease to be at the end of the universal process.

The Old Testament and New Testament Satan is remarkably like Ahriman, although Satan is *not* considered to be so nearly equal to Yahweh (God), except perhaps in the prologue to Job. In Job, Satan (which means "the adversary") comes to Yahweh's (Jehovah's) court as one of the "sons of God" (Job 1:6). He is the great spy, roaming up and down in the earth, seeking out poor sinners to be denounced. Actually, despite this famous passage, Satan plays a small role in the Old Testament.

In the New Testament, *Satan* is a larger, more active

figure.[11] He is the prince of evil spirits, the direct foe of Jesus Christ, whom he meets often in spiritual combat, as in the days of Christ's trial in the wilderness or in the case of his misleading poor Peter, who is straightaway denounced as "Satan" (Matt. 16:23). From this Gospel incident, the early Christians developed a belief that Satan has the power to enter a man and take possession of his life (John 13:27). However, the thrust of the New Testament is that Christ has defeated Satan (the *Christus Victor* Christology). Jesus "saw Satan fall like lightning from heaven" (Luke 10:18). It was death, hell, sin, and the power of the Devil that Christ was supposed to have conquered on the cross. Finally, The Revelation to John (12:9; 20:2, 7–10) tells us of the final punishment of Satan. At the Second Coming of Christ, Satan will be bound and made helpless. After a final battle in which he is defeated again, Satan will be cast into the pit of hell for eternity.

Once there, no doubt, Satan will quote John Milton's tremendous poetry, which makes Satan the hero of the cosmic conflict:

Which way I fly is Hell, myself am Hell; . . . others at last relent: is there no place left for Repentance, none for pardon left? None left but by submission; and that word Disdain forbids me, and with Hope farewell Fear, Farewell Remorse; All Good to me is lost; Evil be thou my Good; by thee at least Divided Empire with Heaven's King I hold.[12]

Apparently, Satan is not one of the symbols that has been seriously damaged by the development of modern thought. Anyone who watches old movies on television will be aware of the number of times Satan as a more or less urbane, sophisticated character appears in the movies of the 1940's and 1950's. The Devil appears in the writings of Stephen Vincent Benét, one of our finest American short-story writers, and is certainly in the background of the metaphysical writings of Herman Melville. The Devil has apparently always cropped up in man's conversation, and the concept of hell and the evil one has never been far from the cursing that forms so much a part of popular everyday speech. Perhaps the greatest enemy of a literal belief in Satan in modern times has been liberal theology, which interpreted evil as an element of the social order, of economics, or even as a psychological phenomenon. It would seem that at the beginning of the 1970's we have moved beyond this form of theology and that there are many signs that Satanism, based on some real feelings that there is a personal power of evil in the world, is alive again.

In the course of researching this book, I was at first amused when some of my students responded with anxiety to the questions I had about the existence of groups of people devoted to witchcraft. I thought that the fear some of them expressed about the activities of some of the people I had learned about in the community was a put-on. Gradually I came to find out that there is a genuine element of fear among some of the hippie-type young people directed toward some of the people who have declared themselves to be black witches and set themselves up to serve Satan.

The most widely known exposé of the developing cult of Satanism in America is the lengthy report given us by the writers of *Esquire* magazine in the March 1970 issue. The *Esquire* report deals entirely with California but I can also add to their information the fact that such groups exist in Kentucky and Pennsylvania as well.

We are entitled to ask, I believe, just why young people in the twentieth century would begin worshiping Satan. What can possibly be an answer? The reasons for this development are complex but generally understandable. The cults of evil are both a reaction to the state of society in our time and the result of the inability of immature persons to deal with the potent tools that science has made all too available to anyone with money.

I do not think we can understand why people give themselves up to a veneration of evil unless we understand that a very great number of young people have come to the conclusion that evil is in control of society. Not unlike certain mystical groups in the distant past, some of these young people seem to have concluded that Satan or the power of evil is winning in the struggle against good and it would be best to be on the winning side. Considering the major questions in our time about our involvement in foreign wars and our ability to extend genuine citizenship to minority groups, we can understand the background of this way of thinking.

But there are far more human and personal problems stemming from the kind of society we have built in America than Vietnam or civil rights. This follows from the affluence of our society and the availability to youth of more money, perhaps, than they may know what to do with. Add to the wealth of the young generation the lure of many new developments in science such as the mood-changing drugs, which encourage the general feeling that if we are bored or upset there is a pill we can take to change that situation, and we have the necessary conditions for the rise of some pretty devilish behavior.

In almost every instance reported by *Esquire* and by the people I was able to interview we find the cultivation of belief in Satan associated with the abuse of dangerous drugs. Perhaps the most common chemical ingested by black witches is LSD. As one of the informants in Tom Burke's article in *Esquire* said:

I've been around that scene, man, cats who have given themselves up to the Lord Satan. If you sense an evil here, you are right, and I'll tell you what it is: too many people turned on to acid. If you make a habit of tripping—well, acid is so spiritual, so, uh, metaphysical, that you are going to be forced into making a choice, between opting for good, staying on a goodness or Christian trip, and tripping with the Lord Satan. That's the whole heavy thing about too many people turned on to acid: to most of them, the devil just looks groovier.[13]

For a number of years, psychologists and law enforcement people have been warning us that LSD is dangerous because it tends to mimic the confused mental state of psychosis. The person under the influence of such a chemical tends to be temporarily out of his mind. Perhaps some of the activity of satanic groups ought to be put down to the acting out of psychoses.

Esquire's articles on the Satan cults made much of a lady who called herself Princess Leda Amun Ra, who is, for all intents, a black witch. In the course of my teaching the philosophy and psychology of religion and getting to know "hip" student types, several black witches have come to my attention. As it happens, both white (good) and black (evil) witches have turned up, as well as some who are not yet sure whether they are white or black or witches at all. Apparently there are a number of young people in the country who *think* they themselves may be witches and are rather desperately searching for certainty. The kinds of things these young people (mostly young women) report as leading them to think they might be witches include experiences of *déjà vu,* precognition of events, and other psychic phenomena, having runs of "bad luck," willing people to come to them, fall in love with them, or leave them alone. Such people commonly report visiting palm readers and fortune tellers who are publicly available for counsel. All report a belief in evil or satanic powers.

Certain other people in or around the hippie-type subculture, either of student age or in their later twenties, have seen themselves clearly as satanic witches. They frequently turn their apartments or "pads" into coven-type witch dens decorated with dolls, symbols, and other artifacts of a blasphemous nature, or at least in very bad taste. Among the artifacts I have turned up are skulls, bones, dolls with painted faces and twisted limbs that are often nailed onto crosses, complete skeletons wired with tiny Christmas tree lights, and old weapons such as knives and swords. These witch dens are usually lighted (if at all) with strobe or black lights, and rigged with record players, stacks of Indian, Japanese, and other strange records, and libraries of paperback books on the occult. The den would not be complete, however, without a supply of psychedelic drugs and marijuana, which is never missing.

Witchcraft[14]

Witches have nothing fundamentally to do with Satan or the Devil, because genuine "witchcraft," a term drawn from the Anglo-Saxon *wissen* (to know), meaning the practices of the wise, had (and has) its own god. This god's name is kept a secret, but he is often represented in the ceremonies of witchcraft as a horned man, or by a man (usually a "high priest") dressed as an animal. In Britain this animal was often a bull, but in France and Germany the animal disguise was often that of a goat. From phenomena like this, along with the "old religion" (a pre-Christian pagan fertility cult that the Catholic Church denounced as demonic), came the common association of witches and the Devil.

Witches and witchcraft represent the remains of a pagan religion that survived in England and elsewhere for over fourteen hundred years after the spread of Christianity to those regions. Indeed, if we can put any credence in the charges of witchcraft brought against the poor souls of Salem, Massachusetts, in 1692, the "old religion" spread right on to the New World. The usual interpretation is, however, that the nineteen people executed at Salem were guilty of nothing but the bad luck of being in the range of some sexually disturbed girls and some even more sexually frustrated clergymen. Arthur Miller has given us a tremendous insight into Salem in 1692 and into the United States as a whole in the mid-twentieth century in his play *The Crucible*.[15] This traditional interpretation of the Salem incident has been challenged recently, as we shall see later.

If nothing else, let us disabuse ourselves of the belief that "a witch is a person who hath conference with the Devil to consult with him or to do some act." This definition, by the way, was the legal definition used in the witch trials of Europe and America.

There have always been, however, and are now *cults* or *groups* of persons, dedicated either seriously (religiously?) or in jest (cynically) to the veneration of Satan or the

Devil, understood to be the chief representation of evil. Without doubt, although our information is meager, there have been black witches (or worshipers of Satan) in Western Europe since the triumph of Christianity in the fourth century A.D. I say *black witches* in distinction from *white witches,* to mean that black witches were deliberately rejecting Christianity and, out of hate of Christ or cynical belief in nothing, sought to venerate evil. The white witches, to the contrary, held to an age-old religion and rejected Christianity not out of hatred or unbelief, but because they had another religion and this religion was a positive, constructive religion that sought fertility and long life and believed in life after death (perhaps in reincarnation) rather than being a dedication to evil.[16]

The existence of *Black Mass* cults and various other orgiastic groups is fairly well established. After the end of the Enlightenment (of the eighteenth century) in Europe, the revival of Romanticism in Germany and elsewhere, and the rise of spiritualism and the various cults of mesmerism[17] in France, there was a skeptical rejection of all that spiritualistic sweetness and light in the form of the "Hell-Fire Clubs" and other downright vicious assemblies of people, especially in Great Britain.

Today, in Los Angeles, the "city of the angels," which Frank Lloyd Wright said is located at the base of the tilt that runs through America, so that everything loose rolls down into Southern California, there is a Church of St. Satan. It is very appropriate, I think, that the religious freedom of the American way of life should usher in the first public, aboveground worship of the destructive power of Satan the world has seen since the Thugs of India were destroyed by the British Army. (The Thugs worshiped Kali, the goddess of destruction.) The "pastor" of St. Satan's Church, Anton Szandor LaVey, has written a very eclectic little book entitled *The Satanic Bible*, detailing his beliefs and practices.[18]

Perhaps this brief indication of the dark side of the current interest in the occult, which must be joined to the rise of the Satan cults and the marriage of magic, drugs, and violence, will demonstrate our need to search for new meanings in the ancient symbols of the occult.

Chapter III

NEW MEANINGS IN THE SYMBOLS
OF THE OCCULT

The thought world of Western civilization has always been influenced by the perennial presence of occult ideas and beliefs. Particularly in eras of religious imperialism —when the church attempted to regulate the beliefs and morals of everyone—men and women, in an attempt to express their innermost drives and desires, turned to the occult practices that survived in the "pagan," or backward, rural areas of Europe for many centuries. After all, the historical circumstances of Europe for the past thousand years or more have fitted the structural pattern that Julio Caro Baroja says must obtain for witchcraft to flourish.[1] Baroja remarks that such a community must have citizens who have been victimized by pestilence, war, and natural disasters.[2] We might observe that certain other conditions must be present also, in that the communities where the occult flourishes generally are rural, even primeval (as in the mountains of Transylvania), perhaps elemental. Above all, witchcraft flourishes where human physical, psychical, and social needs are not met. Baroja says simply: "The world of black magic is the world of desire." [3]

Residual Paganism

Europe did not become Christian all at once, nor did a country become Christian as soon as that faith was accepted by the ruler or the leading people of the nation. Actually, Europe became Christian very slowly, over a long period, beginning with Paul's second missionary journey. Christianity entered Greece in about A.D. 50, and Christianity was adopted as the national religion in Iceland in A.D. 1000. In fact, it was perhaps even later that Christianity really established itself in northern Finland, Russia, and the Baltic areas.

The conversion of Iceland gives an excellent illustration of the true method of the Christianization of Europe. In the year A.D. 1000, the Althing, the Icelandic parliament, declared Christianity the official religion of the island nation. A pagan, Thorgein of Ljosavatn, made the motion that all citizens should be baptized. However, while the island adopted the Christian faith in public, families were allowed to keep some of their previous pagan customs in private. By A.D. 1050, Harold Bluetooth had brought Christianity to Denmark and Olaf the Stout, who brought it to Norway and Sweden, had been converted by Catholic missionaries.[4]

It should be clear, then, that Christianity settled like a veneer over Europe. The "old religions" of paganism simply faded from the official light of day. However, in terms of holidays and special celebrations, such as Halloween and even Christmas, paganism—rebaptized and perhaps renamed—remained a major fact of public life. That the occult still survives after some sixteen hundred years of Christian establishmentarianism should surprise no one.

In Judaism and Christianity too the elements of the occult occur. In Judaism's long history of persecution we see the flight of the persecuted to the mysteries of the Cabala, or storehouse of mystic lore, on many occasions. The influence of the Cabala on Judaism was especially marked in the Middle Ages in Spain, Portugal, Poland, and Russia when persecution of the Jews was harsh.

Christianity often involved practices that came close to magic. There is the anathema ceremony, the laying of a curse on a backslider, mentioned by Paul in Gal. 1:8–9, as well as Paul's reference to the early Christian practice of being baptized on behalf of the dead (I Cor. 15:29). That Christians believed in the reality of demons and devils cannot be denied. The writer of Eph. 6:10–20 speaks of the power of "spiritual hosts of wickedness" in high places.

Alchemy and Alchemists

Alchemy was known to the ancient Chinese and grew up in Europe from the end of the Roman period throughout the Dark Ages, fully developing itself after A.D. 1000. Alchemy was a field of investigation that combined religion, magic, and the elements of physics. Alchemy developed after Europe came into contact with the Arabs, who transmitted to them the secrets of the Hermetic arts. Although alchemy supposedly wished to discover a way to turn "base metal" (lead) into precious metals (silver and gold), it was actually a religion or Gnostic cult, teaching its followers a way of salvation that was at odds with the orthodox Catholic faith that everyone publicly professed. In order to make the magical transmutation, alchemists sought to produce a "philosopher's stone," which may represent either salvation of the soul, in the religious sense, or the union of the conscious and the unconscious, in psychoanalytic terms.

The great Paracelsus (1493–1541) distinguished himself in medicine because he developed empirical researches. He taught, despite his bent toward the "modern" methods of science, that alchemy was "the art of man." He once said, "Be not another if you can be yourself." Jakob Böhme (1575–1624), a deeply religious German mystic, declared the unity of alchemy, religion, and even magic by saying, "There is no difference between eternal life, the re-integration and the discovery of the philosopher's stone." The search of the alchemists, like that of all true philosophers, was inward rather than outward. The psychologist C. G. Jung once said: "The experiences of the Alchemists were, in a sense, my experiences and their world my world. I had stumbled upon the historical counterpart of my psychology of the unconscious. The possibility of comparison with Alchemy and the uninterrupted intellectual chain back to Gnosticism, gave substance to my psychology." [5] Dr. E. F. Edinger identifies the philosopher's stone with the unconscious, the *prima materia* of psychological life.[6] The unconscious, as it receives the devoted efforts of the conscious ego, is helpful to the ego and brings man to fullness of life. In short, the search through magic is the search for one's own fully developed self.

Other Evidences of the Occult in Our History

The terrible history of the Inquisition, which occurred in many places, at many times, was obviously based on belief in the reality of the occult. That there was a Satan, a Devil, and that witches and magicians could work with demons and spirits, was never questioned. The existence of a counterchurch with Black Masses and the Devil as its god was taken for granted. Indeed, the belief of church leaders in such a counterchurch may have provoked such black magic cults into existence.

Of course, there may be a connection, in past history as well as in the present, between abnormal psychological profiles and the resort to occult practices. For example, the shamans,[7] or witch doctors, of Western Siberia are usually chosen because they are unstable and are prone to unusual dreams. These shamans are frequently homosexual and are looked upon as cracked vessels through which the unseen world makes itself visible. The witch, male and female, ancient and modern, seems very likely to be a sexually repressed person attempting to throw off his repressions.

American history shows us the influence of the occult on this continent, and perhaps something too of the negative and destructive power unleashed when men's physical and psychical needs and desires are repressed. The witch-hunts and witch trials of New England grew up in a period after most such activities were ended in Europe. In the context of the straitlaced society of the Puritans, men may have tended to lose their belief in God and consequently to begin to affirm the existence of Satan and witches. Whenever men find it hard to believe in God, belief in the Devil seems to fill the psychological need to acknowledge some power greater than man. In protecting themselves against the powers of hell, the Puritans may have "protested too much," to quote Shakespeare loosely.

The Meaning of the Rise
of Interest in the Occult

For many people today, astrology and other forms of consultation of occult knowledge have replaced the ever-popular Freudian psychology as the means of understanding their own personalities.[8] The value of the more respectable areas of investigation such as Freudian, Jungian, Reikian, and Adlerian psychology seems to have slipped in favor of the tarot cards, palmistry, and the reading of the stars.

The turn toward the occult basically may well be, among other things, an attempt to go beyond the linear thinking and rigid, materialistically oriented logic of modern science and technology to a form of consciousness that grasps man's life in the world in its wholeness. This is the view of the occult movement of youth held by Harvey Cox and Alan Watts.

A view very similar to this is seen among the young people turning to Buddhism. In his article "The Cultivating Scholar," Stephen Lovett has this to say of the young man Ron Epstein, who converted to Buddhism and is now known as Upasaka Kuo Jung:

In the midst of this heavy schedule of study and research he came to realize that the Western attitude toward mind is inexact and superficial in the literal sense of this word, and that he had exhausted the potential of the West in his search for a teacher. His research and experimentation at Harvard had evolved into an interest in the study of certain consciousness realms wherever they might be found. Discouraged in his search for a teacher, he decided to learn Chinese as fast as possible in order to understand first hand the philosophical and religious writings of China. He took up studies as a graduate student in the Department of Chinese, San Francisco State College, and at this time began his cultivation, meditating at the Zen Center in San Francisco.

Not much later he met Tripitika Master Hsuan Hua and began meditating occasionally at the Master's place, listening to Charma although he could not, as yet, understand Chinese. One day as Kuo Jung sat meditating with the Master, he became aware of a bright light radiating from his center, a dazzling light which grew until its brightness obliterated everything.

When Kuo Jung reappeared, he realized that the Master had caused this experience, and knew that he had found his teacher.[9]

As Alan Watts remarks, younger intellectuals are turning to the "masters of wisdom" who form a "magical reaction" against the materialism of modern science. Watts sees this magical reaction among the youthful in mind not as romantic or decadent but as a *human* sort of thing to do. He writes:

Some of our most brilliant and far out scientists . . . [know] that we have thought ourselves through to the bitter end of intellection, or rational calculation, and that, operationally, physics and chemistry imply fall-out, erosion, smog, and ecological imbalance. As H. G. Wells put it, mind is at the end of its tether.[10]

In the April 1970 issue of *Vajra Bodhi Sea,* Dharma Master (Master of the Buddhist Law) Heng Ch'ien, a young American who has embraced Buddhism, writes:

To understand what is outside, you first must understand what is inside. Thus the *Avatamsaka Sutra* says, "Everything is made from the mind alone." This is where the work must be done, in the mind of man. If effort is not applied inwardly man will never transcend his outer environment, but rather the outer environment will overpower and enslave man.[11]

This is very much what Harvey Cox and Alan Watts are saying. In fact, Watts declares:

I am strongly of the opinion that much of this neo-occultism emerges only as wooley-mindedness, below intellectuality rather than beyond it. To go beyond intellection one must practice a sadhana or "discipline" such as Yoga, Za-Zen, t'ai Chi, judo, aikido, or sensory awareness, whereby our consciousness is, at least temporarily, released from linear calculation.[12]

Heng Ch'ien, under the austere discipline of orthodox Buddhism, evidently agrees.

Perhaps this is the most damaging thing that can be said against astrology and the other practices of the occult—their adherents have so little discipline. The very image of play that Harvey Cox invokes for this generation perhaps gives us the key. Nothing in man's history that has proved of worth has come easily; not even religion is an exception to that. To grasp the meaning of his being, man may indeed have to relax and to relearn the joyfulness of childhood, but to understand and participate in the meaning of his being, childhood must end and man must grow up.

The Lure of Eastern Thought

For decades, scholars have propounded the idea that the future of man may well rest upon the successful fusing together of the basic philosophies of East and West. Indeed, from the very beginnings of the modern world's involvement of European economic and military power in Asian affairs, some thinkers have looked to such a unification as the best hope of man's future. The influence of Hinduism, Buddhism, and the several Chinese philosophies of Confucianism and Taoism has been felt in Western literature and philosophy since the early 1800's. As the Western powers moved deeper and deeper into the less technologically "advanced" cultures of Asia, the mystical philosophies of that continent moved deeper and deeper into the Western tradition.

From the first period of Western expansionism until now, the majority of observers have concluded that there is a vast gulf fixed between the religious and philosophical tenets of the West and the East. On this basis of "strangeness" the bulk of Western Christian missionary activity was based. Christianity and the Western empirical way of looking at the world moved into India, China, and elsewhere and sought to convert and displace the traditional Asian way of looking at the processes of life. However, there were always a few thinkers in Europe who were willing to take from the "wisdom of the East." Schopenhauer took from Buddhism what he thought of as a fatalistic appraisal of life. From the East, Schopenhauer thought he was borrowing an acceptance of man's lot in the world, a passivity and calm under suffering and in the face of death that surpassed even the heroic Stoicism of the Western philosophic tradition. Buddha is reported to have said that desire is the root of all sufferings. Schopenhauer said that the *desire for life* is the cause of the rest of man's ills.

Nietzsche too knew something of the philosophy of the

East, and part of his pessimism and contempt for Western Christianity grew out of his interpretation of the Eastern religions. Above all, the *relativity* of religion's ideas was made crystal clear for many nineteenth-century thinkers by their introduction to Hinduism and Buddhism. Oswald Spengler, writing during the depressing and forbidding time of economic disaster and the rise of Nazism, also concluded, pessimistically, that we live during the time of the decline of the West. It seems that the results of the original encounter of the East and the West, intellectually, was an upsurge of pessimism in Western thinkers.

There were real reasons for this historical pessimism on the part of thinkers from about 1800 to 1945. Perhaps the chief reason, even outweighing the political and economic strains and dislocations of the industrial revolution and the many European wars which led on to two world wars, was the comparison between the long history of the East and the relatively shorter history of the West. The sight of a static society in China, five thousand years after the rise of brilliant civilizations there, may have led many philosophers and historians to conclude that such a living death was probably the best the West could hope for in the future, if it did not destroy itself by war over the short run of time.

After World War II a new tendency toward an eclectic unification of East and West appeared. The most popularly known example of this new outlook is that of the historian Arnold Toynbee. In his earliest popularly known work, Toynbee cogently argued that mankind could best guarantee future peace for the world and inner peace for the individual man now by a creative blending of the most positive elements of Christianity and Buddhism. In a series of persuasive writings, Toynbee tried to show the similarities of the highest Judeo-Christian idea of love for fellowman and the noblest Buddhist teaching of compassion for all living beings. Because so many thousands of Americans and Europeans had served in the Orient during the war, and many of them had been deeply impressed by the culture and religion of Asia, Toynbee found a ready audience for his views among the general public, although scholars, from historians to theologians, scoffed at his ideas. Later, Toynbee attempted to express his ideas more critically, to escape the many criticisms aimed at his work.

The Holy Paradox of Religion: Mysticism and Rationalism

Perhaps the most fascinating aspect of Western man's encounter with the religions and philosophies of the East is precisely the fact that they *attract and repel him* at the same time. The religions of the East are often found to revolve around a sense of the "other"—of that which is *alien* to everyday, pragmatic experience—a "sense" of the "nonsensual," of the void, of the *sacred mystery,* of the holy or "wholly other." As Rudolf Otto observed in his ground-breaking work, *The Idea of the Holy,*[13] the experience of the holy involves the paradox of attracting and repelling man at the same time. The holy inspires us to respond in worship but simultaneously puts us off in fear at its alien nature. Man thus loves and fears the situations that make the holy real to him.

Building on Otto's insights, Mircea Eliade writes that Western man, particularly, finds this paradoxical response to the holy unpleasant and unsettling. The ego-shattering humility that such experiences bring is something Western man would generally rather avoid than participate in. The middle-class desire to be safe and comfortable, above all else, makes Western man suspicious of—and perhaps hostile to—any genuine *religious* elements in human experience. It is not only Nietzsche but Kierkegaard and many other thinkers who have observed that the Western middle class has substituted a conventional morality for the essential meeting of God and man in the Christian tradition. But if the religious experience is a necessity for the fullness of man's being, then man will seek *elsewhere* what he does not find in his church or his philosophy. Therefore, the growth of interest in the Western countries in the second half of the twentieth century in the religions of Asia, and perhaps the rise of interest in the occult (the mysterious) in general, may have deep psychological roots.

Perhaps the major strand of thought would hold that man is essentially religious. This is the view held by all parties in the theological discussion that has been going on since the rise of critical scholarship in the Enlightenment period. To be sure, the theological community has been split in the twentieth century between those who see man's basic religiousness as an essentially good feature (e.g., Tillich) and those who see it as essentially a drawback to man's true spirituality (e.g., Barth).

When we turn to the social sciences, there is not the unanimity that one finds in the theological field. Some psychologists such as C. G. Jung see man as essentially religious. Man participates at the deepest levels of his psychic being in the essential symbols that appear again and again in human religion. Jung therefore sees man's quest for wholeness as a spiritual quest, and he is the friend of religion. Other psychologists have not shared his views. As is well known, Freud, at least in his earlier writings, considered religion as illusion and a mark of the deviation of the human mind in its attempts to grasp reality. Man may be religious and yet, for Freud, it is not an essential part of man's being to be religious but rather it is a weakness of man's nature that allows him to be so.

The world of scholarship since about 1960 has responded rather well to the new interests of the generation that I have called elsewhere "the bearers of the new mentality." [14] Whereas before the last decade it was the fashion to overlook the existential, the human interest in the matter under study, and scholars sought to devise all-embracing theories in psychology, sociology, and even in theology, of late there has been a new sociology, a new psychology, and several new theologies. Currently, scholars are becoming aware of the need to remember man's place in the world as well as the human stake we have in understanding our wants and needs as human facts and not just as theoretical data.

Part of the turn toward man and his genuine fears and needs has been seen in the development of the several radical theologies. The "death of God" movement, after all, grew out of a desire to understand the suffering and loneliness of man in the midst of the inhuman events of the twentieth century. The outrage at what man does to man, justifying his deeds so often with semireligious language, lies behind the writings of Richard Rubenstein as well as Thomas Altizer. Again, the desire to form a new theology of hope rests as much upon a deep human desire to enable men to have hope in the face of the threat of nuclear war and the rising fear of racial war as much as it depends upon a desire to interpret the Bible correctly.

If we are to speak of a current interest in religion, we must of necessity be speaking of a different practice of religion than the joining of a church body. The same young people who are so interested in all the aspects of religion are very much disenchanted with institutional religion and pretty much reject even the attending of church. Since the youth of our time find it difficult to trust the people associated with the institutional church, they are more apt to turn to the bearers of new and strange theories than they are to the certified representatives of the traditional religious positions. This means that the average young person would probably take with a large grain of salt the religious instruction available from a pastor or priest and would probably be more inclined to take seriously the teachings of a guru from India or a psychologist who believes man can find his innermost soul through taking certain drugs. Before condemning youth for this kind of gullibility, we ought to recall that it is the church that is responsible for this credibility gap in religion and not the young people. To be frank, it is difficult not to appreciate the reluctance to respect the church on the part of many sensitive young people, and some older people as well, when we realize that the institutional church has either remained silent or has actively supported many totalitarian governments and policies, finding it easy to serve Caesar and more difficult to serve Christ.

The Vacuum in Man's Being in the World

Perhaps the traditional religious symbols of the cross, the blood of the Lamb, the resurrection, and others may have lost some or all of their former meaning for members of both the older and younger generations now living. This is a moot point; the orthodox symbols may or may not have suffered eclipse (in Buber's terms) or died (in Altizer's terms). Yet, despite our assessment of the power still resident in the traditional symbols (and some power is still there), it is a fact that many men and women today are searching for something to fill what they feel is a spiritual vacuum in their lives.

The cinema spectacular *2001: A Space Odyssey* was delightful as entertainment and moving as a projection of man's future expectations in space. I would observe that this movie moves from a science fiction thriller to a religious fiction ecstasy. The theme of the work is rather simple but still somewhat garbled in the film's presentation: Man is not alone on earth, and the space explorers are searching among the stars for evidence that man is not alone in the universe.

Yet, the movie—and the book[15]—does not explore; it assumes. Arthur C. Clarke, basing his projection on the fact that behind every man alive stand thirty ghosts, says that ahead of us, out among the stars, we shall one day meet our equals, or our masters. These masters are almost, if not actually, immortal, and "form" life and intelligence among all the planets of the universe. How close this is to some of the wilder claims of the space-travel groups among the followers of the occult! There are people who firmly believe in the reality of UFOs ("Unidentified Flying Objects")—people including flyers and military officers as well as members of ecstatic religious cults. The "flying saucer" fad of a few years ago was but a chapter in this UFO story. It seems that the usual interpretation of cultists is that more powerful, more intelligent, and more morally good entities are visiting and overseeing the earth. These beings function in the cultists' world view in the same way God and guardian angels do in orthodox theology.

In my previous books, *The Roots of the Radical Theology*[16] and *Radical Christianity and Its Sources*,[17] I discussed the obviously "open" secret that the "high symbol" of God has seemingly lost its power to give meaning and direction to many men's lives. This awareness of the lack of power of the symbol "God" to help men control their passions and emotions has resulted both in the "God is dead" speculation among religious thinkers and in the development of the so-called new morality. Now we can see that this feeling of loss and lostness in the spiritual area is feeding the rising interest in the spiritually ecstatic and in the occult.

Where Religion and the Occult Meet

In mid-1970, the news media began reporting the appearance of a new kind of hippie, a spiritually reformed hippie, known in the crude language of the bar, the beach, and the street as the "Jesus freak." These young people are to be found in small numbers on every college campus but up to now are chiefly seen in California and on small and medium-sized conservative-oriented campuses in the South and Midwest. Such young people have typically experienced a "conversion" from a life bent on sensual pleasure (including alcohol and drug use) to a position exactly like that held by the very puritanical, Pentecostal Protestant sects. Such Jesus freaks are very loud in their praise of the Jesus who has saved them, and they see the world in terms of either/or, black and white; either one is saved or he is not. Worship services tend to be of the loud "prayer meeting" type, with long prayers and, perhaps, speaking in tongues. Older Pentecostals are often convinced of the sincerity of these young people and seem to feel that such experiences are miraculous.

Such a phenomenon in America should occasion no surprise, especially in California, the South, and the Midwest, where the "old-time religion" is still far from dead.

We should also note that in South America, especially in Chile and Brazil, there is a very extensive movement toward religion among the population, but not to Roman Catholicism or the main-line Protestant groups. Rather, conversions are taking place from secularism or nominal Catholicism to *spiritualism* or to the *Pentecostal churches*. Both groups seem to offer supernaturalism in large amounts and to stimulate and develop the emotive life of their members. Men today seem to be looking precisely for that which promises a larger dimension to the world than scientific and economic materialism (either capitalistic or communistic) can give and for resources to feed the emotional sides of their natures.

The Current Struggle Between Jesus and Satan

The rise of the Jesus freaks predates their discovery as a discernible grouping by the mass media, of course. For several years before mid-1970, American popular (or folkrock, acid-rock, and hard-rock) music was showing the struggle taking place between those who looked to Jesus (or white magic, the good) for inspiration, and those who looked to Satan (or black magic, the evil) for the meaning of their lives. The same alienation and insecurities, the same lost feelings and reactions of outrage at the direction of American life, had already crystallized into two opposing forces even among the most "strung-out" of our youth. The lyrics of the music of the Union Gap and the Beatles never stop telling us about Jesus and his love or about brotherhood, peace, and Mary. The lyrics of the Doors and the Rolling Stones similarly seem to raise the power of alienation and Satan to a conscious level.

Our popular singers are more like male and female witches than like entertainers; their lyrics more like the creedal formulations that Arius is supposed to have set to popular music during the Arian controversy in the early church than like romantic ballads. Witchcraft, magic, and religion seem the chief content of youth music today. Reading the words of the songs produced by the Beatles and other groups is an experience that reminds one of reading the book of Revelation. God and the things of religion and the spirit are not dead for the under-thirty group, although the exact dimensions of the traditional symbols are questioned and uncertain. Before the institutional churches and their kept theologians denounce the spiritual ferment among the rock groups, they should recall that the witch (male and female) has had a place in religion from the beginning. Saul consulted the witch of Endor in I Sam. 28:8–25, a passage that probably predates the prohibition of witches in Ex. 22:18. The liberation of the Hebrews from Egyptian slavery took place in the context of magic blessings and curses, and Num. 22:40 to 24:25 tells of the efforts of Balaam, a seer, to curse the Israelites. Balaam tried to do so and could not, for God intervened in such a way that Balaam could only bless the Hebrews (Num. 22:12).

The emergence of the occult in the context of youth culture today might well be seen as a dual sign, demonstrating that there are strains and breaks in our social and psychic fabric, on the one hand, but also demonstrating the relevance of the spiritual *and the traditional* to young people in the McLuhan age. Despite the fact that these young people think they dislike history, and want to live "ahistorically," the lure and power of the traditional symbols of religion and the occult (the archetypal motifs) upon them show us that they are at least unconsciously integrated into the flow of human history. Therefore, the rise of interest in the occult and in the Pentecostal and spiritualistic elements of traditional religion (speaking in tongues, instant conversion, faith healing), so long played down by the rationalistically educated clergy, may be the sign of modern man's groping for a set of meaningful symbols by which to guide his life and give meaning to his activities. As once so many men and women guided the course of their year by the great Christian (or Jewish) festivals and the holy days and saints' days of the church year, so now large numbers of people may be seeking to guide their lives by the advice astrologers and others give—advice derived from the stars, the lines of the hand, or the pictures on tarot cards. Perhaps the advice of the "spiritual reader" is filling the vacuum that is left when men reject the advice given in orthodox sermons.

We all know that Christmas and Easter are very much a part of American cultural life. Indeed, the Christmas season especially is a major contributor to the American economic system. A "bad" business season at any one Christmastime could be very damaging to the economy. Yet, although the business world milks every conceivable cent of profit from the Christmas spirit, no one would seriously hold that the spiritual significance of Christmas gets across to the public in any reasonable proportion to the publicity given to buying and selling of food and gifts. This secularization of the great religious festivals may well be part of the reason for the rise of interest in the occult—as an alternate road to the inner, spiritual meaning of everyday life. To the degree that this factor may be a motive in embracing the occult, we may see the movement toward the occult as an involving motion, a way of becoming more fully a part of modern life. But there are also possible escapist tendencies to be discerned in the move toward occultism.

The Occult as a Means of Escape from Fear in an Age of Increasing Violence

Perhaps at least some of the younger people (and older ones) who have turned to the occult have done so in the hope of finding courage and security in an age of fear and violence. No one needs to be reminded, for example, that this is the century of total war, and that our most disintegrating war (in terms of national morale) has been going on since 1961 and seems to heat up every time steps are taken to cool it down. Soldiers in battle are often highly superstitious, and either out of a cynical sense of humor (common among combat troops) or out of a combination of the two impulses, they often wear crosses, rosaries, charms, rabbit's feet, and buckeyes, while carrying Bibles, letters, and photos—all thought to be lucky or blessed. But in this age of the total electric environment of television and the intercontinental atomic ballistic missile, there is no dividing line between soldier and civilian. With a rising theft and personal-assault rate among our highest crime statistics, we need few reminders of the state of siege under which many urban residents live.

Marshall McLuhan brings this "total war" psychology

to our attention in his *War and Peace in the Global Village*.[18] The age of television-covered limited war and the continuation of the ever-present threat of sudden, total, nuclear war have created—in McLuhan terms—an invisible psychological environment of fear of violence. Perhaps the alienated youth or ghetto dweller who assaults someone else or who abuses himself with drugs is simply showing that he is more "turned on" to the climate of violence than the average, unfeeling man. The citizen who crosses himself when walking home on a poorly patrolled street is reacting to the total environment of fear in a way that, far from being even remotely paranoid, is a true reading of reality in our greatest cities such as New York and Washington, D.C.

Not so strangely, the cults of the occult are strong in our largest cities. Vittorio Lanternari did not carry his great study of *The Religions of the Oppressed* [19] far enough. Many of the Pentecostal sects, the spiritualist churches, and the circles of occult cultists may represent religions of modern citizens of a civilized country who feel *oppressed by the breakdowns and demonic tendencies inherent in American culture.*

On the other hand, the trend toward acceptance of the occult among the young may also be a means of searching for *courage to involve themselves in movements working for social change.* It has, after all, become clear that to involve oneself in movements seeking change in our society can be a dangerous thing. The Black Panthers have been involved in many "shoot-outs" with the police. The antiwar people have had many broken heads and nights in jail. Martin Luther King, Jr., Malcolm X, and many others in the civil rights movement were shot dead. Not all the dying has been done in Vietnam in the last decade.

Could the "put-on" of the hippie cultists who chanted and prayed at the Washington antiwar march, saying they were trying to levitate the Pentagon, have been (like the lucky charms of combat soldiers) at least half serious? Can we be in the presence of a new type of mysticism, a world-oriented mysticism that practices magic precisely in order to involve itself in the life of the world by the doing of potentially dangerous acts—such as participating in a "third world" revolution?

A study of the full dimensions of the occult movement lends credence to the view that there is more than one aim in the new mysticism. Sociological and psychological elements in the rise of the occult mysticism may reveal both escapist and involving goals, just as the culture of those who bear the new mentality shows both active and passive life-styles, as with the hippies and the social activists. The literature of the occult shows us both elements: the escape goal in many of the stories of fantasy, and the active goal in the swords-and-sorcery stories that glory in the help of magic in the doing of mighty deeds.[20]

Chapter IV

POLITICS AND AQUARIUS

Protests as Exorcism

One of the most fascinating identifying marks of the rise of interest in the occult in our time has been the infusion of magic, prayers, curses, and exorcism into public political life. Probably no one could be elected to public office in the United States who did not give lip service to religious belief. A belief in a power greater than man has always, in the rhetoric of politics if not in the direction of public policies, played a role in American life. Never before, however, has American politics witnessed acts of witchcraft and magic performed with a view to changing public policy and the direction of the country.

Norman Mailer has given us a wild view of what he calls "the witches" and their introduction to modern political activity in his book *The Armies of the Night*.[1] Mailer's strange but fascinating half novel and half history gives us the picture of the yippie leader, Abbie Hoffman, and his followers, who presented themselves before the Pentagon on October 21, 1967, with the notion of exorcising that building so that all thoughts of war would leave it and it would float up in the air. Whether or not the young people gathered there took seriously the thought of raising a building is not a problem. Perhaps if you have used drugs long enough you can believe anything. Or, better, perhaps some of these young people might say that magic is no more senseless than scientific and technological thought that does not lead to human happiness but is used to devise instruments of total destruction.

The following are expressions of the kind of politics held by young people who are participating in the Age of Aquarius. These two comments are from students in my classes and reflect a very mild involvement in political affairs by "middle American" students from a conservative area.[2] The first comment is from a young man and refers to the search for meaning by young people:

It seems that man is impelled by nature to seek participation in some greater cause than himself. The intelligent student today no longer finds the society in which he lives to be greater than himself. He finds that the government is no longer in existence for his needs but is rather an oppressor to his freedom, and a destroyer of humanity. Many students today are no longer interested in putting in time in college so they can land that big-paying, prestigious job. Most of the traditional and conventional values of society have become meaningless, and even repulsive, to him. The intelligent, sensitive student learns early in life that the institutions of society are not interested in him as a person, but rather in his category. He goes to school with the mistaken idea that he will be learning through the guided pursuit of his own interest. He finds that he is required to take courses that are designed to fit him into society. He enters the classroom hoping to learn and ask questions, but finds himself cramming for tests and writing papers so that he can be categorized. He is pressured into competition, and concentration on the narrow, assigned studies for the established prize of an A, instead of finding freedom to explore his wider, or special, interests.

Who can the student turn to for guidance or help? The "credibility gap" with the government is so wide that he no longer expects any changes to be made through political means. If he feels he needs help for mental stability, he knows he cannot go to counselors or psychologists, for all they will do is help him adjust to the insane society which he rejected. It is little wonder that suicide is the largest cause of deaths among college students. He needs peace of mind.

A young girl, majoring in German, had this to say:

Student activists feel responsibility for the ills of our society. They feel a sense of duty as citizens of the United States and as members of the human race to make their environment a better place. There is little contentment to be found in dreaming and theorizing. Nor is there peace in turning away or copping out from a troubled society.

Thus their religion is one of action, not one of peaceful meditation. They interpret "peace on earth, good will towards men" as "Let's do something about the war in Vietnam, the children of Biafra, and let's change the idea of 'white men are superior'!" They cannot be content with sending a basket of food and toys to the orphanage at Christmas and then retreating back into their microcosm. For these people need involvement.

They need involvement because it brings them to a variety of rewarding experiences. Not only does it make them feel as though they are accomplishing something;

it also brings the people in the movement together, united by "the cause." It wards off alienation. The feelings of unity ran very high in the march on Washington last fall, as people from all walks of life met to express their dissatisfaction with the war. It is significant that people besides students participated; it shows that others see the importance of their role in our "government by the people." I imagine that the feelings at that march approached the spiritual. For some, it gave a greater spiritual lift than going to church and repeating words.

Students do not merely criticize and tear down. They try to constructively aid the community around them. Students tutor children, help clean up littered areas, help push needed legislation, and participate in VISTA programs.[3]

In a day when it has apparently become a sport for high-placed elected and appointed public officials to bait young people and to provoke them effectively into demonstrations against the sharp turn to the right in national policies, we need to heed the words of this young woman. Students, even the most alienated of them, do not only tear town, figuratively or literally, but for the most part are vitally interested in rebuilding our society.

May, 1970, showed the American public the various ways in which society can respond to student demonstrations. In the case of Yale University, where an explosive issue had developed over the deeply felt apprehension by both youth groups and liberal adults that the Black Panthers accused of murder would not have a fair trial, the mature actions of the campus administration prevented any violence, even though high Washington officials were making provocative speeches about the situation. The Government had airlifted troops to the general area, and the National Guard was on hand, but all soldiers were kept out of sight, and in the absence of repressive measures, the youths' own leaders were able to keep order. A similar kind of demonstration at Kent State University in northwestern Ohio, that one opposing the sending of American troops into neutral Cambodia, was not handled in such a mature way. At Kent State the authorities put armed National Guardsmen on the campus and proceeded to break up the demonstration. Tear gas was fired, rocks were thrown, and suddenly forty soldiers fired into the fleeing students. Four were killed, two girls as well as two boys, and a dozen were injured. The President and the Vice-President said of the situation, in effect, "I told you so." Such actions and attitudes have not gone unnoticed by the young people of America. What is even more frightening to the mature mind is the insight that just such an incident took place against black students at Orangeburg, South Carolina, in 1968, but no large public outcry went up at that time. Perhaps what has happened to our country in the clear turn of our Government to the right, toward authoritarianism, since about 1965 should be more fantastic to the American mind than any attempt to introduce magic into the political process.

Levitating the Pentagon

"The Pentagon," so familiar to us as the name of the central headquarters of the United States Armed Forces, is also the name of a figure or symbol used in magic. Indeed, some critics might say that "the Pentagon," used as the name of a building, is used in a magical way by many Americans!

The Pentagon is a fascinating building. If you have ever

gone to Washington, D.C., by plane, you have flown very
close to it. It is quite visible, sort of shining white in the
sunshine. But entering it is something else! From the air
it looks large, but nothing approaching its true size. Just
getting up to it on the ramps and driveways is quite a
job. Entering the building is a tremendous experience,
something like entering 10 Downing Street and Napole-
on's tomb at the same time. It has its own brand of magic,
not unlike that of the hippies.

Norman Mailer tells us what happened that October
21, 1967, in the confrontation of the two magics of military technology and hippie religion. Mailer, who has
styled himself "Aquarius" since the events of 1967, seems
the perfect scribe to record the occult elements that actually seem to exist in modern American public affairs,
from overseas war to campus disturbance, to peace protest, to sending a man to the moon. (Mailer not only
covered the march on the Pentagon in 1967 but also the
launching of the first manned space flight, which landed
on the moon in 1969.)

Mailer reports that the crowd of young people chanted
"Om" and "Hari Krishna" and evoked every conceivable
deity to purify the Pentagon and raise it into the air. Unfortunately, the Pentagon did not rise up, nor was it no-
ticeably purified of its tendencies toward the use of force.
The magic of chanting met the magic of weaponry, and
weaponry won.

What was illustrated in this encounter—and in the
dozens of encounters on college campuses between students and soldiers since—was the chief problem of our
time, the loss of the inner strength and respectability of
authority. Because the traditional centers of power have
lost so much of their moral strength and possess only

brute force to sustain themselves, men and women of all ages, but especially the young, are now searching for alternative sources of authority—and the occult is one source being searched out, along with radical political ideas. The struggle taking place in the streets of our cities is duplicated on the screens of our cinemas in such movies as *Medium Cool, Easy Rider,* and *Z.*

The Symbol of Authority and the Authority of Symbols

It is a common practice for ministers, college administrators, and Government officials to speak of a breakdown of authority in our day. Every magazine we pick up and half the books we read point out that some very strange things have happened in the twentieth century and particularly in our sector of the last half of the twentieth century. Philosophers, perhaps behind or perhaps ahead of sociologists and political scientists, have begun to study what is openly called the problem of authority.[4] What do we mean by authority? What is it that makes it seem natural for some people in some situations at some times to give directions concerning what is to be done and have large groups of people obey them? Perhaps in the case of pure force, where the directing individual possesses the strength to crush or punish the persons directed if they disobey, there is no problem about authority. Might may not make right, but it does make might, and we have simply a set of conditioned responses working when we have rulers ruling by the size of their fists or the number of their machine guns.

We ought to be quite clear that a breakdown of authority has nothing to do with a breakdown of strength.

In fact, the normal way of observing a societal situation that has undergone a breakdown of authority is to become aware of a significant display of physical force, police or troops, in the conduct of everyday life. For example, the Nazis' rule over Europe was secure in the physical sense for a long time, and the power to maintain their rule was evident by the presence of armed men everywhere. There was, however, a very serious problem of authority. Most thinking people would have suggested that if the question of authority had not been a problem, then the brute force would not have been necessary.

Orangeburg, Kent State, and the Steppenwolf

Hermann Hesse may well be the literary guide to our understanding of the current youth generation, as he is the guide to self-understanding for many youths themselves. Hesse was eighty-five years old when he died in 1962, so he is hardly a member of the present "turned on" generation, and yet, in spirit, he was—and is—one of them. In his own life, one of involvement with Indian and Oriental philosophy, a liberal opposition to Nazism, and an exile in Switzerland from his German birthplace, he was a childlike man, much like the flower child of today.

In Hesse's great novella *Siddhartha* (1922), an imaginative recounting of the life of the Buddha, he showed the peace of mind that can come from renunciation of the treasures of the world. This book gripped the American student generation from around 1964 on. *Steppenwolf*, which Hesse published in 1927, told the story of the "outsider" long before the rise of the French existentialist novelists and Great Britain's "angry young men." The

"Steppenwolf," or "wild wolf of the steppes," is a clear description of the dual nature of man: the one a human nature; the other, a wolfish one. On the one hand, Harry Haller, the Steppenwolf, longed for culture, comfort, and the friendship of other men; on the other side, the wolf in him wanted only to be alone, to be free of the restraints of society, and to fulfill his own desires. Hesse has delineated not only the psychical outlines of the "outsider," of course, but also those of every man—at least of every man intelligent enough and honest enough to look at himself clearly. It is not surprising, then, that the intelligent and sensitive young have seen themselves in the Steppenwolf. In a very profound sense, Hermann Hesse is the earliest forerunner of those whom I have called "bearers of the new mentality."

If the middle-aged generation has its memories of "times that try men's souls," memories forged in World War II and Korea (and for some, in Vietnam), then the new generation has its memories of combat too: Chicago in 1968, Orangeburg in 1968, and Kent State University in 1970. There are many other days of violence on record, from the melees at Florida's spring-vacation beach riots to the street battles over the people's park in Southern California, but these major incidents stand out like Tarawa, Saipan, and the D-Day Invasion of World War II. The wolfish side of the Steppenwolf in all of us has been very evident in the twentieth century.

Brutality, Reality, and the Occult

We need make no elaborate defense of the thesis that the twentieth century has been a time of violence, war, revolution, civil strife, and brutality. Persecution, genocide, mass death by atomic bombs, and massive fire storms caused by "conventional" bombings have all gone to make our time an era when life has been cheap. Faced with the truth of this by the reporting on color television of combat in Vietnam, the Sinai Desert, and elsewhere, and by the actual experiencing of riots and other disturbances in the inner city and on the campus, both the young and some older people are ready to withdraw from the reality that many of them interpret as an inhuman brutality. When that withdrawal becomes important for large numbers of people, then religion and the occult become important too—as sources of escape.

If you think that witchcraft is not widely believed in— at least among the college generation—think on this: A young woman of twenty-one with almost four years of college was so severely troubled over the possibility that she might be a witch that she grasped at the most absurd assurances that the problem could be settled. When told that the general consensus of public society is that belief in witchcraft shows mental disturbance, she acknowledged this and said this is why she tells only a few people of her fears. When calmed by a friend who then "blessed" her and sprinkled her with salt, she reportedly grabbed the salt shaker and poured the contents over her head. Still not completely sure if she was a witch or not, she was relieved by the "blessing" and went away considerably happier.

When we remember that witchcraft (that is, the laying of curses or the giving of blessings) can work if the people involved on both the giving and the receiving end believe in it, we can see the power the occult really has in this Age of Aquarius.

Seen in this light, as an escape from reality, the occult

movement is an opponent of genuine political action—
at least as we ordinarily conceive of the political process.

Kenneth L. Woodward, writing in *McCall's*, March,
1970,[5] tells us that there are "séances in suburbia" as well
as in the East Village. Woodward says that astrology,
tarot cards, palmistry, and neighborhood séances are all
part of suburbia now. The similarity he sees between the
"kids in the village" and the women living in suburbia is
the fact that both groups are uprooted, highly mobile,
and culturally dislocated by the life of our times.

Writing in an article of comment on the state of the
Jewish community in America in the April 1970 issue of
Commentary, Milton Himmelfarb observes:

When people stop being religious they become superstitious, or their children or grandchildren do. Near my
office is a bookshop that has a section for paperback science fiction—or rather, had. You can still find a little
science fiction there, but most of the section is for books
about the occult. . . . Some of the books are *by* witches.
. . . What this may mean was suggested nearly 25 years
ago in a comment about another time—obviously—and
another country. . . . In a chapter on the "War in Europe and the Future of Biblical Studies," W. F. Albright
naturally had to think about Germany: ". . . During the
Weimar Republic . . . anthroposophy and all kinds of
quack philosophies grew apace; spiritism won multitudes
of adherents; the Deutsche Astrologische Gesellschaft had
more members and a longer list of publications than . . .
half-a-dozen scientific societies. . . . Germany was perhaps the land most affected by the spiritual malaise which
swept around the world in that period. . . . The power
of the university élite in Germany was just as illusory as
the power of the French aristocracy of birth on the eve of
the French Revolution."[6]

Himmelfarb is suggesting, as many other commentators have suggested, that the rise of interest in the occult is a sign of the breakdown of society and reveals a degenerate culture. We should not neglect this insight, for it may well be true.

One of the identifying marks of any period that experiences a large degree of interest in the occult is that it is a time when a formerly stable society is breaking up. No one would call the period of the Weimar Republic a normal period of time. Indeed, it is a disturbing period to contemplate, for an ancient civilization that had reached the height of scientific and artistic achievement now was breaking up into rival factions, a situation that would ultimately end with the coming to power of the least civilized elements in the nation. Perhaps, when we think of the Brownshirts fighting in the streets and the use of private armies by all political parties, we can sympathize with the people who tried to escape the brutality of reality (where money was worth nothing and one's life was in danger) by a belief in the stars. The events of the last decade in the United States, while they have not reached the pitch of disintegration that was reached in the internal struggles of Germany in the 1920's and 1930's, do show disturbing tendencies, and this disturbance in society may well be a basic reason for the rise of apocalyptic politics and the search for stability in astrology and the occult.

Seeking to Recover a Sense of History

Many harsh things have been said about the current youth generation—that it is immoral, that it is irresponsible, and that it is unpatriotic, most of which charges

are certainly overstated and could not be held to be true of the vast majority of young people. To the extent that there is truth in these charges, common sense would have to observe that they would be true of only a small number in any extreme form, but that they might form tendencies or themes in the thinking of a greater number of young people from time to time. I would observe, however, that these charges probably miss the point of the really dangerous element that seems to form a large part of the mentality shared by the youth generation—its almost total lack of a sense of history.

It appears to me, on the basis of a decade of teaching in higher education, that this lack of a historical perspective is growing worse with each new crop of freshmen, rather than getting better. By a lack of a sense of history, I mean to refer to the basic outlook of the younger generation that emphasizes the now and is completely caught up in the problems and joys of the present moment. The lack of consideration for those events of both the remote and recent past which have contributed to the shape of the present is a natural enough attribute of the young mind. After all, young minds have just begun to be aware of the events of the world and to begin to hold opinions about what should and should not be public policy. It is a natural mistake to think that the world began when we began to think and get involved, for in a very real and individual way it did—for us. However, the mind that opens itself to the events of the world in a mature way must immediately become aware that we have entered upon a show that is already in progress and indeed has been in progress for a long, long time. We become aware that the good and bad things we find in life neither began today nor will end today; they have a historical past that

we can find out about if we investigate, and they have a historical future that we can project on the basis of the past. Seeing things historically does a good deal for us, for it helps us to be somewhat more objective, and hopefully less emotional, about the evils and the goods that take place all around us.

Seeing things historically, on the other hand, can also be a danger in that it can lead us to an uncritical acceptance of whatever happens to be the case. We may come to feel that whatever is was meant to be, determined by God or history or some other force of fate. Perhaps it is the fact that so many men have shifted their eyes from the freedom of history to the determination of material events and have thus become quietistic (that is, resigned and passive in the face of real evils) that has caused the present generation to emphasize their natural ahistoricity more than past generations have done. This is to say that this generation is emphasizing and developing an ahistorical sense rather than trying to overcome it. This is the reason why some youth speakers can draw such a heavy line of division between themselves and their parents. After all, one often wonders how such a tremendous distinction can be drawn between certain beings and the physical and psychical beings that they have produced— their children.

This conscious effort to live without history, it also seems to me, is the reason for the popularity of Zen and other forms of Buddhism among young people, since Buddhism is essentially an ahistorical form of thought. The *convenience* of lacking a sense of history should not be overlooked, for if we turn our eyes away from the past we do not have to face the fact that we may be part of the problem we are facing or that something that took

so many years to develop as a problem may take many years to solve. It is the kind of unhistorical outlook that often makes the protests and demands of youth groups less possible of realization than they might otherwise be. Only those who are aware of the tortuous course of human events, perhaps, are able to understand just how difficult it is to work out solutions to complex problems that involve millions of people and economic, social, political, and religious elements. A return to the study of history for the insights that it can give, but not from the viewpoint of historical determinism, might be of great help in bringing peace at home and abroad in our countries. The massive surge of middle-of-the-road students and older people to the peace movement after the President's adventure in Cambodia and the tragedy at Kent State may show us an activist way to unite a mature appraisal of history with that pull of the future which is so strong on the youthful mind.

Politics and Religion

As necessary as some form of supernaturalism seems to be to the health of man, and as much fun as there undoubtedly is in the white magic of chanting and attempting to raise the Pentagon from the ground, we must observe that, in the last analysis, the way of politics and the way of the occult are two different ways of approaching the world and can usually only be mixed by missing the point of both activities. The point of view of magic is to control oneself and others by the harnessing of invisible forces, and it is usually made successful by playing on the fears and desires of human personalities; the way of politics is to control others by persuasion in the public

arena. The one works in private, the other in public, although there are elements of privacy and publicity in both. It is undoubtedly true, however, that both magic and politics, as well as religion, condition men to a willingness to participate in much meaningless ritual.

Perhaps the connecting link of politics and magic in our times is the unconscious awareness of many young people that while the external actions of a hippie spellcasting and the rhetoric and hoopla of a political convention are only window dressing, somewhere within the group, and perhaps in a way not responsive to the wishes of either the majority or the minority of those involved, decisions that will affect the course of human events are being made. When men feel that for all their hard work and all their good wishes they are cheated out of a share of control over the destiny of their group, then superstition grows in the area of man's spirit and rebellion arises in the area of man's actions.

Conspiracy

An interesting phenomenon has developed in America over the past few years—the prevalence of the belief that there is a conspiracy afoot to overturn the Government. The charges of conspiracy brought by the Government against the defendants in the Chicago trial of those seven people arrested in connection with the disorders of the Chicago Democratic Convention of 1968 have given rise to the use of the term "conspiracy" by many left-wing groups. Organizations now bear names such as "The Conspiracy Against the Crime of Silence" and "The East Coast Conspiracy to Save Lives." This last group has publically taken credit for destroying draft files and the records of the General Electric Corporation, charging that the real conspiracy in America is that between the Government, the military system, and the giant corporations that grow rich on war spending. The fact is that these groups are very much under investigation and Government pressure. One cannot help noting the similarities between this situation and that of the general war of the church against the "witchcraft conspiracy" in the High Middle Ages and the Renaissance.

We have already noted that the current interest in the occult that is so prominent a part of the scene today is at least partially based on a fascination for the mystery and tradition of Eastern religion. We have suggested also that part of the attraction of the occult is the fact that in it one finds the symbols and many of the teachings of the ancient religions without the disability of the connection to institutional religion which has been so much discredited in the eyes of youth.

We have here what might be called the paradox of the almost impossible combination of a deep spiritual interest and a deep political interest in the minds and hearts of the current youth generation. I have already observed that the aim of the occult and that of politics are two different aims. What can the mixture of witchcraft and political protest possibly mean in any rational terms? [7] Perhaps the occult is not followed for its own sake today but precisely because it is a form of religion that is so much out of the mainstream of the Establishment that it is the only form of religious endeavor acceptable to the politically radicalized youth generation.

The occult can then be seen as a form of man's religious yearning that has escaped discrediting because it is not associated with the main line of authority in America.

It is compatible with politics just because it is by implication anti-establishment, and the practice of it is a form
of rebellion in itself. It is well known that religion in the
West is not historically divorced from political life and,
as many Christian moral writers remind us, religious and
political concerns basically belong together. Seen in this
way, the use of magic as an acceptable form of religion
makes sense and we can see religion in the Age of Aquarius as part of the rebellion of the new generation.

Mysticism and Politics

The fact that mysticism and politics can mix has been
established in history although it has often been noted
that the resulting mixture has not necessarily been good
for the world, as in the case of Rasputin and his influence
on the ruling house of Russia. Again, in the very earliest
days of Christianity's influence on political affairs, we recall that Christian leaders exercised a deep influence on
the mother of the Roman emperor Constantine and even-
tually led the Empire into such controversies over various
doctrines that the Council of Nicaea had to be called.

The influence of mysticism on the political process may
not be as clear and certainly not as direct in the days of
technology and bureaucracy as it was under powerful
royal families. We know that in the ancient days of king-
ship every ruler had his core of advisers, including prophets, astrologers, and magicians. We know that in more
recent times the priests-confessors to queens and kings
exercised strong influences on public policy. Many priests
rose to high office in both church and state and in this
way brought the influence of religion to bear on political
life directly. And in modern times in a democratic coun-

try such as the United States, we have a fairly direct influence of religious thinking upon law and policy with the intervention of Protestant ministers and Catholic priests in controversies over sensitive issues such as the sale of alcohol and the regulation of sexual conduct.

Perhaps the influence of American religion on public policy more correctly ought to be called moralistic rather than mystical. The objections of many Catholics to governmental activities concerning birth control, however, might be better understood as the result of belief in mystical doctrine, such as the joining of the soul to the body in the womb, rather than as expressions of moral feelings about the taking of life and the responsibilities of sexuality.

We have an even clearer picture of the direct influence of religious thinkers on the political process in America at the present time. Undoubtedly the tragic failure of the attempt to enforce morality by the prohibition law caused a setback to those who would make their religion more influential on the political process. But the failure of prohibition also had the salutary effect of driving the more rigid religious thinkers from the political field and giving liberal ministers a chance. I am referring to the fact that the Congress of the United States and many state legislatures now have a number of clergymen as members. One of my own seminary classmates is a member of the legislature in the state where he serves as a pastor. One of my seminary student friends is taking a year off from his religious education to stand for the state senate in his home state. This kind of activity has been very successful in recent years and appears to be increasing.

We must also speak of some of the demonic effects of the influence of mysticism upon political leaders and the political process. We need not go back to the czar in Russia or to the Roman Empire but simply note the fact that Hitler appears to have been a believer in occultism and consulted an astrologer about the prospects of his plans. Again, outside the realm of the occult as such but still reflecting more superstition than mature religious insight, we must note the heavy influence of fundamentalist Protestantism on many of the politicians of the Deep South. There are still many so-called ministers of religion (not limited to the South alone) teaching the discredited doctrine of racial superiority by reference to Old Testament texts taken out of context. These doctrines often provide philosophical justification of the attitudes and actions of bigots among the electorate as well as in public office.

Since we are dealing with fundamentalism, without opening up the whole subject of radical right-wing activity, we must mention the fact that there are a number of so-called religious groups such as the "Christian Crusade" (previously, "Christian Anti-Communist Crusade") that teach a form of superstition that has been destructive of goodwill and reason in public affairs for a long time and appears to be gaining strength today.

Suggested Alternative Futures

The second half of the twentieth century has given rise to the study of the possibility of predicting alternative futures for society. The proposal of alternative futures for man is probably older than a written literature itself, and goes back into the period of human history in which the transmittal of culture was done by means of oral tradition. In a sense, every prophet that has arisen in human history (even in protohistory, before things were written down) has given man a set of alternative futures and demanded of men that they choose wisely among them. The message of the prophets of the Old Testament, both of those who did not write and are reported on only long after their lifetimes ("the former prophets") and those who either wrote themselves or were recorded by disciples ("the later prophets" or the "writing prophets" such as Amos and Isaiah), was essentially one that gave Israel and Judah two alternative futures and demanded repentance by priest, king, and people if the more frightening alternative was to be avoided. The prophets used more than simple fear to put their message across, of course, and pioneered in the use of satire, parable, metaphor, and myth to make their point.

The satirical writers of later times really followed in the train of the prophets. Juvenal, the great Roman comic poet, raised social satire to the status of a high art in his stinging comment upon Roman manners and morals.[8] Juvenal's first book, *Satires I–V*, was published about A.D. 110 after he became sick at heart over the debased morals and literature of his day. He brilliantly answers the question, "Why write satire?" in a poem that hits on and at every pretense and racket that Roman (and any urban) society produced. As he says:

> . . . To priority over the sacred offices.
> For by all the gods,
> Majestic mighty wealth is the holiest of our gods,
> But as yet, pernicious money, you inhabit no shrine
> Of your own, we've made no altar for you as for the
>   benign
> Old deities peace and honor, virtue and victory,
> Or the one where storks croak answers to prayers—
>   Harmony.[9]

That could as well be said about our day as Juvenal's!

However, it is more likely that our age needs less a satire on morals than one on our surrender to the method of science as the answer to the problems of human life. An earlier period of the twentieth century has given us some brilliant examples of what a satirical (and frightening) treatment of alternative futures can be. Aldous Huxley's *Brave New World* [10] and George Orwell's *1984*,[11] along with Ray Bradbury's *Fahrenheit 451*,[12] are among the best of these prophetic attempts. Huxley, more than most, looks beyond the fascination of the 1930's and 1940's with science to see the possibility of a soulless Eden, a sterile society without human interest, at the end of a technologically developed, "planned" society.

Recently one of my students, a physics major with a minor in philosophy, remarked about the current search for meaning among college youth:

The first, and probably most important [of the reasons for a desperate search for meaning on our campuses] is the mental atrophy and gradual expiration of an old man named Science. It was this man who in his youth caused the deterioration of the church and much of Western tradition while he was converting the world. In his later days he reared a handicapped—blind, deaf, mindless, and soulless—son, whom he called Technology. This son now allows his father to continue living, but only to do his bidding. This, the clinical death of science, has removed one of the great sources of meaning in the lives of contemporary students, that was enjoyed by previous generations. University students no longer feel they can, through practicing the cult of science, make the world a more fit place to live—not in the least estimation. Many students are of the opinion that the opposite effect will result.[13]

Another student, also a physics major with a philosophy minor, says:

It is quite possible that what is termed as a search for meaning may be a result of what our scientific age has done to the standard means of searching for this type of meaning. In ages past when one felt that his life was utterly meaningless he would go to two possible sources to find some meaning: the church or philosophy. These provided meaning throughout the ages until the scientific revolution relegated both disciplines to the realm of irrelevancy. Men soon found that both of these classic sources of meaning were far outstripped by the method and scope of modern thought. It seemed that all things had meaning in the great order of the universe except the creature called man, and that slowly but surely his meager place in the order would be supplied by a cybernetic device many times more efficient than himself.[14]

This sets the stage for what is happening at the present time.

Long ago, the satire against religion began. One of the earliest known representations of the crucifixion shows a crude human figure with the head of an ass nailed to a cross. Anatole France, in *Penguin Island,* satirized the Christian missionary impulse in his story of some naturally innocent and intelligent penguins who were converted and thus thrown into confusion by their new knowledge of good and evil.[15]

Now the age of the satire of science is in full swing, and in a much more violent form than the rather mild fun-poking of *Science Is a Sacred Cow.*[16] Aldous Huxley reentered the lists against the uncontrolled advance of scientific technology with *Brave New World Revisited,*[17] written in 1958, twenty-seven years after the writing of *Brave New World* (1931). In this very pointed critique of Western culture at mid-century, Huxley tells of the dangers to the human spirit brought about by overpopulation, overorganization, propaganda and marketing advertising, brainwashing and the use of drugs and subconscious persuasion —all aspects of life today. Against these new forms of the demonic, the youth of today are protesting in their criticisms of the civil rights policies, foreign policies, and systems of national priorities of the Federal Government. The various youth (and older liberal) groups that sponsor protests against the war and establish environmental awareness seminars are actively striving to offer America some viable alternative futures. Perhaps, however, the more fantastic alternatives shown us by Heinlein in *Stranger in a Strange Land* [18] and by J. R. R. Tolkien in *The Lord of the Rings*,[19] with their emphasis on the feeling of being an outsider in the world and on the heroic quest for meaning, speak more directly to the youth of today than do even the most radical political platforms.

Considering the shading off of youth along a continuum from Heinlein's and Tolkien's books (which they treasure) to the most bizarre practices of the occult, reality may be more fantastic than we imagine. There are stranger things than are dreamed of in academic philosophy.

Chapter V

SEX, DRUGS, EMPIRICISM, AND MYSTICISM

I believe it to be quite accurate to say that the present-day college-age and young-adult generation is absolutely familiar with the phenomenon of drug use. I have noticed a distinct change in the attitude, and frankness, of the college student over the last decade on this score. Despite the fact that the use of marijuana and the psychedelics and "body" drugs such as heroin is illegal, there are few young people who have not "experimented" with such substances or else know other young people who do. Without defending the use of these substances in the least, I simply want to point out that we are fooling ourselves if we think that our present public and legal attitudes and machinery are discouraging the growth of drug abuse.

Present-day young people start the drug habit early, undoubtedly because the sight of their parents using so many prescribed drugs for psychosomatic and emotional disturbances has conditioned them to think that happiness means a pill. Max Metcalf, a Lutheran pastor working with county prisoners on Long Island, has this to say about the suburban addict:

Drugs used by the young people in the suburbs are mostly stimulants (amphetamines) and sedatives (barbiturates).

These drugs are pills which are swallowed, not shot into a vein. They are used to give a varied state of very intense elation and very intense suppression, not depression. Youth take alternate doses of stimulants and sedatives, trying to achieve a controlled, manageable, and fluctuating hypersensitivity. As one young addict explained to me: "If you mix the ups and the downs together, it gives you a racing feeling inside. It's sort of like racing the car engine with one foot on the gas, and keeping the brakes on with the other foot. It really churns you up inside."

The psychology behind this middle layer of addiction is a peer group action, not the individuality of the heroin addict. During the initial experimental period, youth usually use either cough syrup or the marijuana reefer. Graduation to the pills comes quickly. They are taken just before or during a party, in order to get high. The tablets or pills are consumed with soft drinks or beer. The mixture of beer with the drugs is supposed to give an extra high and a better kick. Usually this type of addiction is a group action involving those who would otherwise have great difficulty functioning in group activities. The person who has difficulty relating to others tries to overcome his fears with drugs.

There is also an anti-social side to the psychology of this type of addiction. On a one-to-one basis, these drugs often are used to make another person "fall." Dozens of times in group counseling sessions, I have heard addicts admit they deliberately went all out to tempt or coax another teenager into taking the drugs. Why? "Just to see them fall, the way I did!" The stimulants (amphetamines) are also used as a sexual stimulant in one person's conquest of another. They are in frequent use at sex parties.[1]

Over and over, the same story that comes to a pastor, teacher, or other person trusted enough by youth to be sought out as a counselor: experimentation with drugs, trouble with parents, problems with school work, and very often problems arising from casual sexual contacts, such as unwanted pregnancy or venereal disease. One young lady from the South told my secretary that she was worried because she was pregnant and her parents were coming to visit her. When advised to tell her parents everything, she declared, "I would, but it's so hard to tell them that the baby will probably be black."

I have often wondered why there are so many unwanted pregnancies among young people when there are so many mechanical and chemical techniques to prevent such things. I have at last decided that the reason must be that the effect of one kind of chemical cancels out another. I am afraid that under the influence of pot or some other dope most young people never think of the consequences of sexuality and consequently take no precautions. By the same token, no thought is given to the possibility of infection or disease. Consequently venereal disease is on the rise and is strikingly high in incidence among the very young of high school and college age.

Living Aimlessly as a Rejection of Western Empiricism

It may well be that the reasons for so many unwanted pregnancies and the rise of the venereal disease rate stems from the same attitude on the part of the young that leads to the hippie style of life and social activism in behalf of idealist causes. A life led without regard to the prudence that is so clearly the main nerve of middle-class thinking may be the desire of many young people who would rather take the chance of physical and social problems than live cautiously in the way they see their parents and teachers living. This rejection of the rule of care and prudence over their lives may also be a basic reason for the acceptance of drug use and the following of astrology by many youth. Being intoxicated on a drug puts one in a very nonprudent position and makes one's frame of mind loose, free, and generally aimless. Following astrology provides one with a form of guidance that removes some of the anxiety that must come into personalities so far removed from the usual order of things. On the other hand, since the guidance given by astrology or other occult practices does not make sense to the "straight" mind, the occult does not make the student or dropout feel that he has sold out by seeking such guidance for his life.

Recently one of my senior students had this to say about the need for guidance in life and the attraction of astrology:

Each person, regardless of how weak or strong, seeks a guiding force in his life. Some so desperately reach out that they may grasp at anything and only too soon become dissatisfied and reach out again. He may move discontentedly from religion to alcohol to drugs and so on. Astrology has recently become extremely popular among many kinds of people. Last year millions of dollars were spent on astrology. Thousands read their horoscopes each day—some amused by it, some dependent upon it to tell them each move to make, and some used it very effectively as a sort of guide.

To me, astrology is not so much a prophecy of fate, but a reminder of so many of the possibilities in life. On occasion, it may help one proceed more cautiously than ordinarily, to look for hidden opportunities, to be more thrifty, or any of a variety of helpful hints.

I must admit, though, that I feel a bit strange when I

read the horoscope for the day before and find a striking "coincidence." For example, about a week *after* I applied for and secured a position at a Lexington hospital, I read that day's horoscope—"an excellent day for seeking out new job opportunities." Weeks after I set my wedding date, I checked the horoscope for that day. The ceremony will take place just minutes before the moon moves from a position good for solemn promises, etc., to an excellent position for lavish spending, gay festivities, etc.—the reception and wedding trip. These are only two examples that have led me to feel that in some way, the order and movement of the stars do have some influence on each person's life.

That there are forces beyond man seems likely. Obviously, if events can be foreseen in time and space, then these events come into existence independent of man's limited world of time and space. Something must be organizing this system and administering it for our benefit, since we certainly are not doing it ourselves.

Man essentially must earn his advancement through his own efforts. He can be helped through superior forces, if he is receptive and they are willing, but unless he has also exerted maximum effort, he is bound to fail.

At times I can hardly believe that there is organization to any of this chaos. Sometimes I can hardly gather enough faith to trust in or believe in anything or anyone. Usually what helps me through these times is remembering that it's not a matter of how the stars move or how God plans things but the way in which I deal with it. So astrology may be one end to a search for guidance, but it is how one accepts and uses this guidance that really makes the difference.[2]

Dr. Donald Nugent, of the University of Kentucky, has been investigating the phenomenon of the occult for some time and has zeroed in on the involvement of youthful interest in the occult, seeing it as connected with the abuse of sexuality. In a recent speech entitled "The Future of Witchcraft," Nugent observed:

There are other areas where elements of the youth revolt, however justified and praiseworthy, have some congruencies with and can shade off into the rise of witchcraft. Unrequited love is readily metamorphosized into hatred or reduced to lust, as some sink in sense [i.e., into sensuality] as the only way out. Some seek to overcome the paralysis of the will by exploring ways in which it can be artificially or magically heightened. Sex is enlisted in the struggle, as the act of love becomes an act of resistance— even violence. "Groupies" ask to be flagellated. Cleaver, an admirable and tragic spirit, wrote of rape as "an insurrectionary act." The "Foreplay" to *Che* announces that "the flesh crucible investigates the erotic clairvoyances of political irrealities." This kind of thing is suggestive that political frustrations are being translated into a ritualistic sexuality, and this is suggestive of witchcraft.[3]

There is no doubt that the practice of witchcraft in either a serious or a playful manner is tied up with some rather obsessive sexual practices. A characteristic of the young people who are involved or leaning toward involvement in satanic groups is extreme interest in participation in casual sexual relationships. Within the black-magic cults, one finds homosexuals at one end of the spectrum and girls apparently with nymphomania at the other end. Without doubt, the idea that joining such a group will give freedom and cover to socially frowned upon sex practices leads many to join such groups. There is much evidence to support the belief that the use of aggressively offensive language such as four-letter words has always played a part in the underground cults that have been associated with witchcraft and the Black Mass. The recent rise of emphasis on filthy speech may be an outgrowth of the recent rise in the interest in black magic, or it may be a source feeding the development of such ideas. We know from an investigation of materials on witchcraft from the seventeenth century that what today would be considered unprintable words, except perhaps in *Playboy*, occur in the literature as part of the beliefs of and about witches. Certainly after discounting a good bit of the sensationalism spoken of about witch meetings, there must be a residual element of truth to the report that a good deal of sex play went on at these midnight meetings.

The $64 Question: Is Witchcraft for Real?

Chadwick Hansen, in his significant study *Witchcraft at Salem*,[4] says:

The traditional interpretation of what happened at Salem is as much the product of casual journalism and imaginative literature as it is of historical scholarship. It might be summarized as follows: (1) no witchcraft was practiced in Massachusetts; (2) the behavior of the afflicted persons, including their convulsive fits, was fraudulent and designed chiefly to call attention to themselves; (3) the afflicted persons were inspired, stimulated, and encouraged by the clergy (especially Cotton Mather). . . . Yet the facts are quite contrary to these common assumptions. To begin with, witchcraft actually did exist and was widely practiced in seventeenth-century New England, as it was in Europe at that time (and still is, for that matter, among the unlearned majority of mankind). It worked then as it works now in witchcraft societies like those of the West Indies, through psychogenic rather than occult means, commonly producing hysterical symptoms as a result of the victims' fear, and sometimes, when fear was succeeded by a profound sense of hopelessness, even producing death.[5]

Thus Hansen holds that there was witchcraft at Salem, and that there is witchcraft today, wherever it is believed in. My experiences among the present-day college generation and my memories of the beliefs of people in the low country of South Carolina where I grew up lead me to agree with Hansen's thesis. To answer the question bluntly: There is such a thing as witchcraft; it exists and it works. I have seen the fear that it inspires in college seniors enrolled in large universities, fear that passes over into clinical paranoia in some instances.

A colleague interested in investigating the occult with me recently wrote the following about a student informant who had helped us a great deal: "Joe Dokes called and said he wants out of further 'witch-hunting' on X Street. I don't blame him. His every third word was 'paranoid.' I think he should cool it and rest." [6]

To be very frank, witchcraft rests upon acceptance by those who know of its teachings and rituals. It operates by suggestion and its suggestibility power is quite strong. To those of a passive disposition, the pressure of curses, spells, charms, and rites is too great to resist. Witchcraft is a question of mind over mind, and I have seen it work on white, middle-class, well-educated people in the heartland of the United States.

Fear of an Unknown Hex

A young lady was once referred to me for pastoral counseling by her roommate, who feared she was "flipping out." It soon became apparent that this young person was living in a state of extreme anxiety over the possibility that someone (unknown to her) had laid a hex, or curse, on her. Her fear had its foundation in a series of tragic events. Two of her boyfriends had been killed in automobile accidents. Being extremely attractive and quite popular with young men, she was the object of a good deal of envy by some of her less beautiful classmates and knew it. After the death of her second boyfriend she soon came to the tentative conclusion that her life was under a curse. She feared that any young man she might fall in love with would also die. For a time she tried to shun boys, but her normal vivacity and healthy interest in the opposite sex, and their undoubted attraction to her, soon made her spinsterhood impossible. She began to "steady date" a husky young man on the college football team, a man who looked as if he need fear nothing. But the affair was afflicted with problems from the start, since the young woman felt that if she allowed herself to fall in love with the boy, he would be killed too. She told him of her fears and he at first laughed at them and tried to talk her out of such nonsense. Little by little, however, he grew uneasy and also became anxious. He stopped laughing about the hex, and after three months the relationship was broken off. They continued to date "just as friends" once a week afterward, but when the young man was involved in an auto accident, although he escaped injury, he fairly obviously began to believe as intensively in the young woman's hex as she did herself.

At the last counseling session the young lady resisted all attempts to give the events of her life a rational explanation and announced the intention of "giving up men" for a long period of time to see if that action would lift the curse. Attempts to refer this person for psychiatric help were resisted. Witchcraft seemed stronger than pastoral counseling and, on the basis of other cases, I would observe that it may be stronger than psychiatry. I base this rather wild-sounding judgment on the fact that a young M.D. preparing to intern in psychiatry who was asked to help me in the counseling of this young lady refused on the grounds that such things as curses frightened him. The doctor wasn't at all sure that the young lady wasn't right in her suspicion. Perhaps more people should read Hansen's book and take it seriously.

What Is Involved in a Voodoo Death?

Medical science has long recognized that there is such a phenomenon as "voodoo death" or death from extreme anxiety brought on by the fear of witchcraft spells and curses. While the phenomenon is not fully understood, it is well recognized and documented. Several theories have been put forward to explain these deaths, among them the following:

We must bear in mind that in a society which believes in witchcraft, it works. If you believe in witchcraft and you discover that someone has been melting your wax image over a slow fire or muttering charms over your nail-parings, the probability is that you will get extremely sick. To be sure, your symptoms will be psychosomatic rather than organic. But the fact they are obviously not organized will make them only more terrible, since they will seem the result of malefic and demonic power.[7]

The Phenomenon of Voodoo Death[8]

Medical authorities for centuries have recognized that certain highly suggestive personalities can be literally "frightened to death" by stronger persons who lay "curses" on them. Essentially, the phenomenon of voodoo death is an example of "stress death," stemming from the glandular and organic changes brought about by a continuous, sustained state of acute anxiety. The adrenal glands are overstimulated by the presence of this acute anxiety, adrenalin flows through the system, the heart begins to beat faster and faster and may go on to develop abnormal rhythm patterns that can lead to death. In some cases of stress adaptation syndrome (known as SAS), anorexia nervosa,[9] or the hysterical rejection of food and consequent onset of starvation, may set in. Motor aphasia (aphemia), or the inability to speak or at least produce an articulate sound, may also occur.

A milder phenomenon, *bolus hystericus,* or the "lump in the throat" that can lead the person in a state of extreme anxiety to feel that he is choking to death, or being choked to death by a demon, is also well documented. Hansen reports that the records of the witch activities in Salem contain many references to this experience.

The choking sensation we shall find over and over again; it is the *bolus hystericus* and is related to the "lump in the throat" felt by normal people in moments of extreme stress. The normal person, like the hysteric, tries to relieve it by swallowing; this is why the comic strip artist has his characters say "gulp" when they are in trouble.[10]

The connection of such hysterical syndromes with problems of personal identity, self-confidence, and a comfortable, well-accepted sex role should be obvious. In the affair at Salem, several young girls, just passing into womanhood, were afflicted with witch's "curses." Among these were Mary Warren (age 20), Mercy Lewis (age 19),

Mary Walcott (age 16), and Elizabeth Hubbard (age 17). Among the signs discerned on the body of Sarah Good, who was accused of "tormenting" the girls, was the report of her own husband that Sarah had a strange tit or wart on her person, which was interpreted to be a "witch's tit" at which the Devil was supposed to drink the witch's blood.

Bruce Handler, of the Associated Press, recently reported on the *Macumba* or "Black Spiritualism" cult of Brazil in a newspaper story. Handler was able to attend a "service," or séance, in a slum apartment in São Paulo, where the following episode took place between a middle-aged woman and her two teen-aged daughters:

About five minutes later, there was a shrill scream. To my astonishment, the mother also had become possessed by Tangazu. Her formerly serene face tightened into a hideous glaze. Her eyes rolled up. She, too, dove to the floor and started chanting in the same mushy-mouthed language her daughter had been using.

With the mother now the center of attention, the daughter in white retired to a corner and slowly descended from her possessed state. Her hair lay back on her head. Her eyes opened. She wiped the sweat from the bridge of her nose, smiled and began speaking like any normal Brazilian teenager.

The mother, still in a possessed frenzy, came to tell the fortune—through Tangazu—of the daughter in white. It was hard to believe that a few minutes earlier that child had been practically in another dimension.

"Does my new boyfriend like me?" the girl asked the spirit.

"He does? Oh, I knew it!" she shrieked, her face lighting up.[11]

There is every reason to believe that the lure of the occult is at least partially tied up with a quest for sexual identity and sexual satisfaction. We will be able to document this more fully in the following pages.

Sex and Mysticism

Donald Nugent, well qualified to interpret historical phenomena and sensitive to the fine points of theology, has given more weight to the appearance of witchcraft in our time than most other commentators, including this writer, have been willing to give. Nugent mentions the significance he sees in witchcraft and the rise of the belief in Satan in an interesting article, "The City of God Revisited," in the Summer 1969 issue of *Cross Currents*.[12]

Specifically, Nugent sees witchcraft and the occult as an inverted form of mysticism. Again, he sees interest in the occult as related to human sexuality and thus of a piece with the broad *Playboy* Philosophy of our times. What is more exciting, he very clearly sees and establishes a connection between witchcraft and political involvement.

Nugent first of all views the rise of witchcraft as a mark of the return of mystery to the human consciousness in our time. He quotes with approval, although critically, Norman Mailer,[13] who has written in several places about the confrontation of the hippies and their exorcism with the Government at the Pentagon demonstration we discussed in Chapter IV. What is at issue is the insight of both Mailer and Nugent that for whatever reasons we may finally establish, the generation now coming to maturity cannot live as so many of their elders do live without the depth of myth and symbol and the richness of mysticism that marked human life centuries ago before the rise of the empirical, or scientific, attitude. Mysticism, these rather unintelligible rites seem to be sayng, is back and will be around for some time to come. It may not yet be clear what influence such mysticism will actually have on the political process, but that it will have some influence seems indisputable. Perhaps, its major influence—and a healthy one if it is possible of attainment—will be the creation of a climate of opinion among the younger people of America, and of the world, that demands and expects every human effort to be made to reach and preserve a state of peace. Of course, here the mysticism of the young will be very close to the central stream of mysticism as seen in Judaism, Christianity, and the great Asian religions such as Buddhism, all of which preach peace as the ultimate social good.

Nugent sees the relationship of witchcraft to religion and to sexuality as being very closely intertwined. In a way, Nugent believes the appearance of interest in the occult even in its most questionable forms such as the Satan cults of California and the reported group sex of groups of occultists who practice black magic in England, is a positive sign for religion. This is to say that the appearance of interest in Satan negatively implies that the religious dimension is not and cannot be dead but is still active in human society and that with the revival of belief in Satan we must expect a revival of a belief in God. Another religious plus that Nugent sees in witchcraft is the fact that taking the Devil seriously means taking seriously one of the fundamental Christian doctrines, the reality of sin and the seeing of evil as a real possibility in the world. The doctrine of original sin and the teaching of the reality of evil were out of fashion for a long time in the twentieth century. The appearance of the witchcraft cults therefore signalizes the end of that period of shallow liberal theology which was unable to deal with the problems of Nazism and racism.

A renewed intellectual recognition of the problem of what Kant called radical evil could only be of benefit to the world. Insofar as the rise of interest in the occult makes the question of the reality of evil topical, we may conclude that whatever other values there may be in the movement, it has made a positive contribution to the maturing of thought in our time.

The Spiritual Dimension of Human Sexuality

Religion has always taught that sex is more than a physical process. In the religion of both the Old and the New Testament and in the extra-Biblical faiths such as the worship of Baal and the other fertility cults of history, sex has been seen as the expression of invisible spiritual forces at work in the world. Against the secularism of modern times, which would see sexuality as simply an instinctual drive or as the mindless response of one set of glands to another, religion both pagan and Judeo-Christian has always held that the physical is but one dimension of the whole experience of sexuality. Many writers in the twentieth century have documented the meaningless drift of people who have lost all sense of the spirituality of sexuality. Perhaps the most literate fictionalized account is *Couples,* by John Updike.[14] An excellent survey by a minister is the report on spouse-trading, pornography, and the *Playboy* Philosophy entitled *The New Immorality,* by Brooks R. Walker.[15] To the degree that the rising interest in witchcraft is truly an expression of the younger generation's belief that there is a mystical element in sex, then witchcraft has to be seen again as a positive thing.

Donald Nugent sees witchcraft as very much an outgrowth of youthful revaluing of sexuality. Regardless of what this revaluing may be doing to the responsible use of their sexuality, and Nugent does not believe that it is a good thing, we may see sex and magic as youth's way of connecting the Western outlook to Eastern mysticism.

Nugent observes that there may be more sex than love involved in the highly trumpeted love philosophy advanced by the hippie movement during the past decade. He rather wisely observes that the love of the love generation could not have been the ideal love taught by Christianity or the compassion of Buddhism since so many members of this generation quickly moved away from an emphasis on nonviolence. As he says, the "Student Non-Violent Coordinating Committee became violent, or some of the gentle sex became castrating Amazons." [16] Nugent even connects the recent interest in the use of bad language, as seen in the free speech movement, with a kind of word magic, reminding us that the Biblical names for Satan contain reference to human excrement and that the use of such crude terms today might be an unconscious attempt at using the language of devil worshipers.

Nugent compares the liberated or free-form expression of sexuality among the younger generation today, with their accepted styles of living together without marriage, a growing incidence of group sex, and the general feeling that what one does with his own body is nobody else's business, with witchcraft. Apparently Nugent has accepted the historical charge of the Catholic Church that witchcraft was the expression of perverted sexuality and the worship of Satan instead of God.

Of course, many writers on witchcraft very much deny that witchcraft has been only a rejection of the Christian

God in favor of the Christian devil. And these same writers, while recognizing the basis of the ancient witch cult in the fertility rites of prehistory, deny that it has ever been a question of sexual immorality. Pennethorne Hughes, writing in *Witchcraft*,[17] and Gerald Gardner, writing in *Witchcraft Today*,[18] both hold that the charge of the Catholic Church that the witch cult's worship of Satan was immoral was an unfounded attack designed to discredit what they call the "old religion." They do offer the view that the god of the witch cult was often represented by a man wearing a headdress featuring large horns and that reports of the appearance of such a person at coven meetings may have led to the identification of the witch-god with the popular image of Satan as a horned being. It is also historically established that the goat with large horns played a significant role in the ritual of the witch cult.

One must bear in mind the reasoning of writers who have attempted to rehabilitate the old religion of witchcraft before taking as a proven fact Nugent's thesis that witchcraft equals free sexuality. Nevertheless, it is probably fair to assume that sexual attitudes in the witch cults were freer and less repressed than was the attitude of the church of the Middle Ages. Considering that the Catholic Church, as well as many conservative Protestant churches, still holds very strict views on sex, we may see in witchcraft even today a more casual attitude toward sex relations than we see in the church.

Youth, Sexuality, and the Use of Drugs

We have noted in previous chapters the close relationship in the hippie subculture between sexual casualness and the use of drugs. It should not be surprising to learn through such news reports as those about Charles Manson and the violent group associated with him, as well as the articles in the March 1970 issue of *Esquire,* that those groups of witch cultists which have deliberately turned toward black magic are heavy users of a variety of drugs and the practicers of unusual sexual customs. These published reports have been verified by me in conversations with young people who have come into contact with black witchcraft groups in cities scattered across the country. My reporters say that the people they have met who fall into his classification are "sick" and seem addicted to sadism and masochism. They also report very irresponsible attitudes toward the taking of the most dangerous drugs and severely aggressive feelings on the part of these cultists toward "straight" society. I would have to conclude that many of the members of these black-magic groups are ripe candidates for psychological treatment and are probably potential violators of the criminal law.

If the connection of drugs and sex were made only by Satan cultists, we would simply leave the problem to the psychologist and not see the issue as a moral and religious one. However, among the members of the youth generation, both within and without the subgroup of young people interested in the occult and specifically in witchcraft, there is a widespread connection between frequent and casual sexual contacts and the use or abuse of drugs. It is not the case that every party at which young people gather to smoke marijuana or even to ingest stronger drugs turns into a sex party. Conversations with young people have convinced me that participation in illegal activities such as use of marijuana does not break down the overall moral code of the person involved, especially with regard to sex. On the other hand, many pot parties or trips with LSD do involve sexuality of either a public or a more private nature.

I have slowly formulated the opinion over a number of years of interviewing people and doing a good bit of personal counseling that those who are casual in their sex relations will be that way whether they are taking drugs or not and that their casualness in this matter probably predates any drug experience at all. By the same token, those who are more responsible in the sexual area will probably continue to be responsible whether or not they ever participate in drug use. I would want to exclude from this opinion persons who are very, very young and inexperienced and who may not realize what they are getting into when they experiment with drugs (the so-called teeny boppers), as well as persons who might be considered of a low order of intelligence and persons afflicted with such severe psychoses that they are unable to take a responsible attitude toward sexuality or any other area of human decision.

I suppose that this insight, if it is genuine, goes against the generally accepted view that the abuse of drugs, even of the relatively nondangerous marijuana, leads to moral breakdown and particularly to the ruin of the moral character of young girls. I think that the connection of promiscuity and drug abuse is a parallel one to the expression of alienation or of searching by personality types who are unsettled and have no clear sense of their own identity. I do not think that there is a before-and-after causal relationship between either the use of drugs and then sexual promiscuity or the abuse of sex and then the abuse of drugs. In other words one does not necessarily lead to the other, nor is it necessary that a person who indulges in one of these activities goes on to indulge in the other. It will depend upon the inner dynamics of the personality involved. A person having a strong moral code with regard to sexuality but suffering from some internal need for fulfillment may experiment with drugs without going on to sexual promiscuousness. On the other hand, as is well known, there are many people now (as there have always been) who have engaged in a multitude of sexual relations without ever turning to drugs. I think it is important to see the true connection between these areas of problematic human conduct.

The Influence of Eastern Mysticism on Current Concepts of Sexuality

Sometime ago *Playboy* magazine ran an article on Japanese views of sexuality, illustrating it with art prints of a high quality. The theme of Oriental sexuality ran through the series of prints, and yet the emphasis upon the erotic was more physical than mystical, as if the editor assumed that a Western audience would be more interested in the physical than the spiritual. That probably was true some years ago, but anyone making that assumption today, including a *Playboy* editor, would be quite wrong.

Much has been made of the casual sexuality of the hippie groups and of the high school and college age young people who have adopted their life-style, with the usual implication that this is a hedonistic, erotic generation. To some extent that implication is true, and yet the hedonism of the now generation is spiritual too. It has its meanings and its own codes, although perhaps a

review of one of the Eastern classics that has influenced
this generation, the Hindu scripture called the Kama
Sutra,[19] will help to make the mysticism of youthful
sexuality today a little clearer.

The Hindu Ritual of Love

The Kama Sutra is a classical Hindu treatise on love
and the conduct of relations between men and women
in society. It chiefly directs its attention to the conquest
by the male of the female. It is divided into seven parts,
with thirty-six chapters that cover in detail the means of
wooing a lover, the actual touches and embraces of love,
and the various sexual positions that bring pleasure and
fulfillment. The young people who congregate in places
like the East Village and the "Hashbury" area of San
Francisco are often seen reading this book.

To be brief, the aim of the Kama Sutra is to instruct
the interested person in the various techniques of attracting the opposite sex and then making him supremely
happy. This is important because the young people
today seem to be well aware of the selfishness of sexuality
that is so widespread among the members of their
parents' generation.

Perhaps of far more importance with respect to current views of sexuality is the characteristic of Eastern
thought that is able to preserve the very old in a living
tension with the new. In this regard, the philosophies of
China and Japan are perhaps more explicit than the
thought of India. Particularly important in its influence
on the young has been Zen Buddhism and the Taoism
of China. The feature of this Far Eastern thought that
most appeals to the young is the vision of the world as

forming an interrelated community in which man and nature are not just externally, but organically, related. This is a kind of pantheism that conceives all things, even the most physical of things, as spiritual.

To the degree that the young people of our day have felt alienated from their bodies and from the world around them by the linear thinking of the West, they have gladly embraced the Eastern view that heaven, earth, animals, and men form part of one large, living whole which is very sensitively interrelated and which is progressing toward the triumph of spirit. Seen in this light, the statements of young people that they take drugs in order to experience the wholeness of being begin to make sense. If we keep this unitary point of view in mind, we can understand the oftentimes garbled reports of those who have taken LSD that "it is all one," that "all is God," "there is nothing to worry about." It may be that Timothy Leary is not wrong in drawing a heavy line under what he sees as the connection of mystical or religious experience and psychedelic or drug experience—at least for the younger generation. Alan Watts has also made a rather close connection between the taking of drugs and religious experience, particularly of an Eastern kind, in his book *This Is It, and Other Essays on Zen and Spiritual Experience.*[20]

Recently a graduating senior student of mine, definitely one of the new generation with an experimental attitude and a way of life and dress that sets him apart, took as his senior research project the study of the philosophy of intuition of Henri Bergson. This student saw the real possibilities of Bergson's philosophy for students today and made the connection to Eastern thought and drugs in the following words:

With the current popularity of Eastern thinking, and the mind-expanding philosophy of Alan Watts, one may find the intuition of Bergson to be more relevant today than when it was written. Whatever the intimate essence of that which is and of that which happens may be, Bergson says that "we are of it." This statement . . . seems to be very much like the themes of Watts's essays, being mostly of the nature of the self and intuition. Anyone viewing linear-type thinking as inadequate for a true picture of the Self and the world may find Bergson's philosophy to be as satisfying as the philosophy of Watts.

Alan Watts is also an experimenter in the new alchemy of mind-expanding drugs. I am sure no one knows just how the mind functions, but it is theorized that certain chemicals operate upon the nervous system by reducing some of the inhibitory mechanisms which screen our sense-data and so select only some of them as significant. I feel certain that many new discoveries and insights will be made with the continued experimentation with these drugs, but if the effect produced by these chemicals is anything like an intuitive insight, Henri Bergson's intuition of real duration may be very close to what in fact is the case. With these drugs (LSD, etc.), objects do appear to move and secondary qualities (colors, etc.) change with the succession of inner psychic states. As Alan Watts said of one of his experiments: "I became vividly aware of the fact that what I call shapes, colors, and textures in the outside world are also states of my nervous system, that is, of me. . . . I was the sensations, so much so that there was nothing left of me, the observing ego, except the series of sensations which happened—not to me, but just happened—moment by moment, one after another." These series of sensations have to be grasped, as Bergson said, intuitively; for when one tries to use reason to stabilize or understand how a qualitative state or change came about, the next change has occurred. When one tries to use his intellect to grasp this flow of sensations, he becomes like the frustrated dog trying to catch his tail.[21]

Perhaps as a final illustration of the current youthful view of drugs and drug experiences as mystically religious, we might offer the following quote from a young person interviewed by Max Metcalf:

One young inmate who claimed he had taken more than 100 LSD trips explained one to me:
"I took the acid, sat back on the bed with the record playing wild, exotic music. In about 20 minutes it began to start. I got up, looked in the dresser mirror, and saw myself turn into a candle. Then I began to melt down into a little puddle of wax on the floor. I could see bright, iridescent colors of smoke, and I could taste the music—like salt and pepper. Then I seeped under the door and floated down to the beach. There suddenly the clouds parted and I watched my soul leave my body and go up through the hole in the clouds—and there I met God. He took my soul to the planet where it will live when my body dies from life on this planet. Man, was it a beautiful place. . . ."
When I tried to confront this young LSD addict with the reality that it was only a chemical inducing a fake vision inside his brain, he replied: "Who cares about that? I can't wait until I get out of jail. When I do, I'm going to take an overdose—because I want to go back to that planet God showed me . . . man, was it ever beautiful!" When I next tried to confront him with the danger of death from an overdose, he replied: "Yeah, but what a way to go!" [22]

We would have to see this young person as being an extremist, to be sure, and yet the general thesis put forth, that one can see a better world under the influence of drugs, is more widely spread among young people perhaps than is the use of strong drugs themselves. Max Metcalf remarks that the psychology of the psychedelic drug addict is one of a religious nature, and yet he feels that the use of such psychedelic drugs is perhaps best understood as an escape from a society that has prolonged adolescence so long for the college student that adulthood seems uncertain.[23]

In summary, it would seem that at least some of the reasons for the turn of many younger people toward the mysticism of the Far East and India, as well as for the increased emphasis on sexuality and the use of psychedelics, basically grow out of a general feeling of anxiety and insecurity. This insecurity is seen by many psychologists and sociologists as having its root in the structure of the present-day society. Perhaps we need to see it as caused by the sense of meaninglessness and the thirst for spirituality of sensitive young people who have been starved for a comprehensive vision of the wholeness of being by the lineal thinking and positivistic philosophy of the twentieth century. The current interest in the occult is connected to a desire to escape from the confinement of the empiricism of the West, which is drying up human imagination and sensitivity to such a degree that many young people feel that *1984* is not a harsh enough critique and has already occurred.

Chapter VI

EXTRAPOLATIONS ON THE FUTURE

The recent rise of interest in the occult makes the question as to the probable future of religion quite relevant. It is, after all, possible that occultism might, like the buds on a rotting potato, drain all the life and substance out of the body of organized religion and leave it an empty shell. Of course, there are many entirely sympathetic observers (as well as despisers) of religion who would hold that organized religion is an empty shell already.

Ramifications of the Rise of the Occult Today for the Christian Church

Donald Nugent has observed that the future of the church will be muddied and blurred for some time to come. That is a safe observation. He points to the already present blurring of the lines between the sacred and the secular, a blur already seen in the "pop" worship services of young people on their spring-break beaches in Florida and in the involvement of churches in credit unions, picketing, overseeing Government grants in ghetto areas, and other activities. The rise of such groups as the Native-American Church (for the religious use of psychedelics) and the many "mail-order churches" with their legitimate "ordinations" (which many hip people are buying!) does have some ominous meaning for the traditional organized religious groups.

Nugent further has observed that a young people's "be-in" or "happening" can be seen almost as a witches' sabbat. More to the point, he can see mysticism (both Christian and Eastern) and witchcraft as inversions of each other. He observes that the Gnostics had a myth that Christ and Satan are brothers, and even Christ connected the serpent and the dove in one of his parables (Matt. 10:16). Nugent suggests that mysticism and witchcraft are species of the famous coincidence of opposites that plays so large a role in mystical theology—as well as in ancient, pre-Socratic, and Chinese philosophy. Therefore, the appearance of witchcraft in modern society is the sign of a growing movement toward mysticism in our time.

Nugent's analyses are brilliant, and yet I cannot help thinking that his connection of witchcraft and sexuality—or should I say, oversexuality—mentioned in his paper "The Future of Witchcraft," discussed earlier, is not so much wrong as it is one-sided. Of course, witchcraft and the occult are connected to sexuality, but mysticism—and religion itself—may well be connected to sexuality too. (There isn't a whole lot in human experience that isn't.) Nugent observes that sex today has been enlisted in the struggle to resist the trends of American society, so that the act of love is now seen as an act of violence. We could interpret some statements of radical youth leaders in this way, but I see no evidence that such a view is widespread. It may well be that it is the failure of most church leaders, teachers, and lay members of churches to be fully honest with themselves and others about their own problems with sexuality that is doing the most to drive the church away from youth and into a supporting position for economic and political reactionaries. A recent report made on the basis of a six-month study of the prospects for religious publishing concluded (among other things) that people are buying books on the occult in great numbers and not buying religious books. Since book buyers are generally older people, we might conclude that even the older Americans of today are trying to tell the church something.

The Need for the Church to Get with It

One of the clearest warnings to the established church that I can see in the recent rise of interest in the occult, the continuing experimentation with drugs, and the ongoing sexual revolution is that if the church as an authority doesn't "get with it," then its future is bleak. Anyone who thinks sex is dead or that the sexuality of this generation is just the "old immorality" is quite mistaken. What people today are looking for are *not* the scientific techniques to increase mere sensual stimulation (more orgasms for women and men) but precisely for the mystical "more" in sexuality taught by the Kama Sutra and other mystical traditions. It seems clear to me that aware, concerned men and women of all ages will more and more turn to the occult as it becomes clear that their organized churches are purely rationalistic and have accommodated themselves to the economic needs of the state and the logical positivism of scientific thought. These aware people will use the economy and the scientific techniques of the Establishment to neutralize the power of the Establishment over their lives, if not to destroy it. A study of science fiction, and especially of science fantasy and the sword-and-sorcery novels of today shows us precisely these themes.

A real example of this subversion of the repressive external order by use of its own powers is the widening use today of a drug that has been around since 1941, MDA.[1] MDA is known among the hip young as "the love drug." This little capsule is often quite small, with a cloudy-white top and clear-white bottom, revealing a white powder within. The drug is *meta diox. amphetamine,* and it produces dilated pupils, numbness, and an increase in interpersonal relations without arousing sexuality.

Although it is frightening to think of, and at best a half truth, it is the case that there is a chemical basis to life and that man has brought himself to the position where he can chemically transform himself without going through the agony of discipline and the struggle toward maturity that the world has always demanded for wisdom up till now. It is partly true that drugs can change man's thinking and external behavior. MDA shows us that; so does the reality of the mixed technique of psychology and drugs that we call brainwashing. But what is chemically transformed is only that dimension of man that is chemically transformable. We may change our moods so that when we are tired we can take a pep pill (as many middle-class people now do), when we are nervous we can take a tranquilizer, and when we are ready for sleep and too tense to sleep we can take a sleeping pill. But, even with more sophisticated drugs that not only can control the functional illnesses that come from too rapid a pace of life but can also control more serious pyschoses, such temporary relief cannot bring genuine healing to man, nor can it, above all, bring to him wisdom and a sense of the meaningfulness of life.

The realm of wisdom, the dimension of compassion, the area of genuine love, is not an aspect of man transformable by chemical means. Not even a better, more fully developed MDA can give maturity and a genuine sense of compassion based on the fellow feeling of a person who has loved, worked, fought, and suffered through years of experience. MDA can give the feeling but not the substance of compassionate love. In this area, those who, from the standpoint of the older generation and representing the state and the organized church, maintain that the way of drugs is not the answer for man's search, are right. In this respect, those among the members of the new mentality who stress the need to find one's meaning through contemplation, meditation, prayer, and good works, including social activism, are right. Already the fact that the way of drugs is not the way to a meaningful future has established itself in the minds of all who will listen. Even the relatively recent usage of MDA has impressed upon young people who have tried it the fact that its effect of giving one a feeling of brotherhood is transitory, lasting about six hours, and bringing with it the side effects of nervousness, anxiety, and physical exhaustion. This fact demonstrates that it is not the way to genuine lovingness.

In drugs and in selfish sex, as in a life of interest in personal gain and pleasure, the result is finally a sense of discouragement in the person, regardless of age or status, whether he is a businessman or a college revolutionary. Discouragement becomes a sign of the negative meaning of life, for discouragement is the feeling of disenchantment with love of self. Our ambition to succeed, either in the traditional way or in the radical way of finding self-understanding, turns to envy of others who seemingly have found more peace than we—an illusion that obtains only because we do not know the inner life of the other. The mistaken goals we follow bring us to discouragement. The sense of discontent with our lot in life and the resentment we feel against others who do not share our restlessness bring us discouragement. This discouragement then expresses itself as mistrust and worry when we think about the meaning of our unhappiness and this further deepens discouragement.

Finally, self-love turns sour, turns to anger, first against ourselves, then against others, and sparked by any external pretext turns to violence either against ourselves in suicide or against others in physical assault. We may control these tendencies for a very long period of time with drugs, but the day comes, or that hour in the middle of the night, when we must face the world alone without our crutch. Like the drunkard without a drink, in that hour the emptiness of our spiritual dimension, no longer covered over with drugs or sex or anything, opens wide and swallows us in its void.

I have suggested that man has a residual dimension to his nature, lying more profoundly deep in his psychical constitution than even the biochemical dimension of his total mental-physical self. I would, personally, call this dimension spirit, but I would not object to any other term, including "life," or the Bergsonian "*élan vital.*" Whatever we call it, even if we consider it to be purely materialistic (as in the medical view that the use of chemical transformations simply "wears out" the nerve fibers so that one's responses to the world are blurred, and that only long-term experience, where stimulus-response patterns are laid deep in the nerve tissue, can bring true knowledge), it is still clear that man cannot save himself by any shortcut—no matter how scientific.

The Future of Religion

Recently I reviewed Passolini's *The Gospel According to St. Matthew* and was struck again by the relevance of the Gospel story to men in our day. Out of the seared and pitiable soil of Sicily, out of the weather-beaten faces of the Italian peasants, and out of the literal, straightforward retelling of the story of Jesus the Son of Mary, the Italian Communist Passolini, with his passion for the poor and suffering, made the Christ live again. Disregarding all the scholarly studies made over the centuries and the so-called "modern" attitude that there are no miracles, Passolini gave us Matthew's Gospel, miracles and all, without comment. The symbols of new life out of death were simply laid before us—and surprised us with their power.

I think that faith in God not only is possible for the young (and young in heart) of this generation but is an inevitable fact of their experience. I think that for the first time in living memory the more educated and more sophisticated of our youth are taking God, the Spirit, Christ, and Satan seriously. But before we begin building church buildings again, let it be clearly understood that these young people are not necessarily "turned on" by the church's proclamation of faith, nor are they likely to join institutional churches. Much more likely is the development of a loose, "latent-Church" [2] movement with speaking in tongues, faith healing, spiritualistic séances, literalistic Bible-readings without scholarly comment, and street testimonials. This "church" will not be doctrinal or rationalistic in any sense—it will put a premium on the emotional, the sensitive, and the experimental. It will represent a return to the sense of mystery and the emotional in religion. *It will undoubtedly be called a revival of paganism by the organized churches. But what's in a name?*

Perhaps, looking at the need for the revival of the sense of mystery in religion, we need to ask the more basic question first: What does it mean to be religious?

Whatever else it means to be religious, it must mean that one's vision of life is more than a positivistic approach to things. It must mean that one accepts the reality of something more than that which can be seen and handled, tasted and touched, measured and weighed. It must mean, in a sense, that the depths of things are not open to man and that they contain in a paradoxical way the meaning of man's being.

To be religious must mean that we find release from the up-till-now prevailing Western emphasis on consciousness and rationality and find a way to put ourselves in touch again with the unconscious portion of the human mind. To be religious must mean that we have passed beyond the psychologizing of everything in terms of the unconscious or the biologizing of everything in terms of the process of evolution and the rationalizing of all our experiences in the broad, catchall explanations that attempt to tame everything and make it familiar and comfortable. To be religious, in short, means that we will not reduce the mysteries of life to mechanistic laws that take the life and the adventure out of everything. Until we hold a sense of mystery and feel that we are involved in an adventure that is leading us onward in an eternal quest to understand ourselves and the universe of which we are a part—until then we cannot be religious and the occult will rise up to more clearly put this vision of the world before men. Insofar as the occult makes life an adventure and a quest and is not taken as a sense of escape, the occult functions as religion and is a good thing. To the degree that the occult is not a quest but a form of escape, man's future is in jeopardy and we can expect not only the expression of the underlying nature of man (which would be to man's good) but also the expression of irrationality and the demonic in the form of self-destructive behavior in men and in nations.

Perhaps the religion that is alive today in the hearts and lives of people is a truly pagan one rather than the religion of the Hebrew-Christian sources, although the symbol of Christ (and especially the symbols of Christ's suffering and his humanity) is very much alive among the young. But the symbols of Christ have seemed to be alive at many times and places, precisely among those who are otherwise estranged from organized religion. We have mentioned the deeply moving portrayal of Christ in the film by the Communist Passolini. We also must note the recent film from the state cinema of Communist Hungary, *St. Matthew's Passion,* which presents the singing of this wonderful music against the background of films of the Nazi nurder of six million Jews in World War II. It would be hard to find more significant and essentially religious statements of the meaning of the crucifixion in anything done by the church. Perhaps the appearance of these films is an example of the insight of McLuhan, who has through his writings put forward the thesis that there are unconscious forces, perhaps of a symbolic nature, working on us through our mass media and technologies.

Men today yearn for an element of the supernatural in the affairs of everyday; they struggle to create openings in their lives for the experiences of mystery, adventure, and romance in the midst of the routine tasks of our society. They drive too fast on the streets and highways, flirting with death—the last mystery, which even our science cannot completely overcome. They seek out other men's wives to give an element of risk to otherwise drably safe (in the short run) existences. In the afternoons their television sets are tuned in to comic attempts to re-create the fantasy of werewolves and vampires on the *Dark Shadows* series; at night they titillate themselves and their girls with double-feature horror movies at the local drive-in. They decorate their apartment walls with posters such as the fantastic "Mother Earth" drawing, which shows a man copulating with a tree. They search out their horoscopes for the day and walk through the paranoid city, suspicious of everyone around them. They are looking for peace, but the television only tells of more war. They are looking for health, but the radio only tells of cancer from cigarettes and cyclamates and of heart attacks from too much fat in their diets. They are looking for home but cannot go home again because urban renewal has leveled it or their parents live in retirement villages. They go to church and Christ's miracles are explained away in the sermon, and the taste of the well segregated wine in separate cups turns sour on their tongues.

Since the reality in which we live is viewed as this kind of spiritual desert by millions of young people (I read the above paragraph to a group of university students just after writing it and they all exclaimed that this is precisely the way they see our society), it is not difficult to understand why many people may turn to occult groups. At the same meeting at which I read part of this material, some students told me of the existence of a fabulous voodoo cult that is flourishing among young, white, middle-class people, not university students, in a Southern city in one of the border states. Perhaps the reader would be interested in the description of such an occult group.

The Setting and Decor of the Occult

Imagine yourself walking down a major street of a medium-sized city with fewer than one hundred thousand residents. A small, very well known liberal arts college lies on your left; to the right opens a sedate residential street. You turn right and walk under the graceful old trees that line the sidewalk. On the right is a brick bungalow, the home of a nationally known psychiatrist. Just down the way, the chairman of a department of a major university makes his home. Hardly the place to go witch-hunting? Hardly, and yet across the street, one house down, is the location of a coven. Five people—three men, two women—and all of them witches.

We cross the street and climb the stairs of an old mansion whose air is one of tiredness. It is not a run-down building. The house is painted and swept, but its glory is gone. Now it is divided into apartments, two up and two down. We go upstairs and knock at a door. It opens at our rap, of its own weight. The door is not locked, nor has it a lock at all. The rooms of the coven stand open to the world.

What rooms these are! There are five rooms, all differently decorated. In the room we enter, dolls, painted and distorted and torn, are hanging everywhere. A crushed skull stands on a shelf. A coffee table supports a birdcage in the middle of the room. Inside the cage is a painted doll rather than a bird. From time to time someone takes a sword and "torments" the doll, all the while calling it Cosmic Charlie.

One corner contains a fireplace. A gas-log fire is burning there. Several other persons are seated in front of this fire, "grooving" or "flashing" on the flickering gas-light—for the people in this room are almost completely "stoned," or intoxicated on drugs.

Someone greets us and hands us the skull. This is a grotesque item, old, brown, with the jaw missing and with a crushed-in line running from the right eye to the top of the skull. The boy who has given us the skull tells us that it is the remains of a murder victim, dug up in an adjoining city by black cultic friends who sent it on to them as a present. We are offered a pot cigarette, decline it, and wander to another room.

Walking through the crowd of guests in the dim light, we are struck by the wild expressions on the faces of some of the people present. A tall, beautiful, black-haired girl sways back and forth as if hypnotized. Incidentally, some of the guests are rather distantly "tripped out" on LSD.

The next room is brightly painted and at first reminds us of a little girl's room. There is one significant difference—all the furniture in this room has been very carefully bolted to the ceiling. Brightly glowing, hip colors cover the table, four chairs, dishes, silverware, glasses, and flowers that hang suspended from the ceiling. This witty, amusingly decorated room lightens our outlook, and some of the sense of evil that we felt in the other room falls away from us.

The next room returns some of that foreboding, because of its color as well as on account of the direction in which it drives our thoughts. It is a small room, painted completely black; a deep, ebony, shining black, from floor to ceiling. Only one object is in the room, a brass bed; all of it is painted black too, except for the large rails at the head and foot, which glow richly in the light falling from the next room. There are no lights and no other objects in this "bedroom."

We walk back toward the front room and become aware of exotic music coming from a record player hidden somewhere in a dark corner. A few of the people in the larger room are moving back and forth to the music, dancing or "grooving" to the weird sounds. From their behavior, we would judge that at least some of these people are homosexuals.

Among the things mentioned by the people at this party was their connection with other black occult groups in neighboring cities. The characteristics of the cult members seemed to be the following: All of them are young, under thirty for the most part, with high school and some college education. Almost all are now out of college or high school and working at white-collar jobs. All seem to be single, but many are living together, often with several men and women sharing the same apartment. The use of wine, beer, marijuana, and drugs, as well as psychedelics, seems to be universal among them. While totally alienated from the society in which they are located, they seem to be apolitical. Each person seems turned in upon himself or herself, fascinated by the internal contradictions he finds within himself. Their philosophy of life is best described as a sensationalist hedonism. For them, evil is more fun than good, and a great pleasure is derived from shocking and frightening the more passive types of hippie students who live in other apartments in their area. One very upset hippie type who visited the coven says he believes they would like to make a human sacrifice, just to see what that trip would be like.

A Mystical Look at America

Another student, remarking on the fascination of astrology and Chinese philosophy for this generation, had this to say:

In the Zodiac, the Gemini myth corresponds to the Yang-Yin disk. The symbolic twins, of the Gemini myth, are both divine and mortal, and black and white. One creates and the other destroys. They represent creative nature (*natura naturans*) and created nature (*natura naturata*). The Gemini, in essence, is a symbol of inversion, of opposites in its dynamic aspect. (White tends toward black, night seeks to become day, the evil man aspires to goodness, life leads to death.) It is a symbol of the harmonious ambiguity of thesis and antithesis, paradise and inferno, love and hate, peace and war, birth and death, praise and insult, and clarity and obscurity. Here, gay matters are discussed in grave tones, and the most tragic events are joked about. If this cosmic situation were worked out in psychological terms, it would mean that the zone of contradiction (the center of the Yang-Yin) would become the threshold of unifying and unified mysticism. This would explain the abundance of contradictory epithets in the most sublime poetry, and the extraordinary richness of paradox in the deepest thinkers such as Lao-Tse.[3]

The same student, applying the symbols of Eastern religion to the present-day United States, has this to say:

Although they do not even rank as amateurs compared to the Hindus of India, Americans regard themselves as highly accomplished in the art of loving. Symbolically their concern with the bi-unity of the sexes is expressed in many ways. I don't believe any interpretation is needed as to the symbolism of the Washington Monument, and the placid waters of the moat in which the monument is reflected, expressing the union of the two sexes. Although the monument's reflection in the moat's waters is symbolic of both sexes, the United States is definitely on a masculine, aggressive trip. Nature is conceived as feminine. Before civilization came, America, the place, the land, harbor, and river, are clearly marked as female. It is both pure and wild in its untouched state. By implication the masculine society later dominates and controls it. The Yankee City of progress is masculine-dominated, its culture is masculine, and its significance and achievements are masculine. From masculinity, presented as powerful and full of prestige, flowed the events that molded the life of the society; in it were contained the superior and authoritative virtues. In general, woman's position was dependent and given little interest or attention. In this collective rite there was little excitement in seeing or being a woman of Yankee City. The audience was meant to attribute its feelings of value to male, not female, images. The predominant symbols of the U.S. are the powerful bulldozer and the rocket (that great phallus which blasts the skies).[4]

It seems to me that the responses of these young people to our society (the descriptions of the spiritual barrenness of our society, and the insights of the above-quoted young man, for example) make it very clear that any religion that will be viable in the present or the future must be one of mysticism, mystery, communion, and oneness—in other words, a form of pantheism or, better, panentheism.

The Religion of the Present and the Future: Panentheism—A Melding of Paganism and Revealed Religion

Pantheism is as old as the original religious philosophizing of mankind, although it had its chief philosophical development in the works of the great thinkers Benedict Spinoza (1633–1677) and Gottfried Wilhelm Leibniz (1646–1716). The American philosopher Josiah Royce (1855–1916) developed the doctrines of pantheism to a great extent for the people of the twentieth century.

What Is Pantheism?

Josiah Royce, writing in *The Religious Aspect of Philosophy*,[5] describes the doctrine of pantheism as the view that God is the whole of reality. As Royce puts it, "All truth is known to one thought, and that Infinite." All human activity is the progressive realization by men of the eternal life of an Infinite Spirit, Royce says, following the philosophy of Hegel. He further declares, "Live out thy life in its full meaning; for behold it is God's life." God is everything, and everything is God, if men would only become aware of that, according to the beliefs of pantheism.

What Is Panentheism?

Panentheism, according to the analysis of Charles Hartshorne and William L. Reese in the volume *Philosophers Speak of God*,[6] means the doctrine that holds that *God is eternal—temporal consciousness, knowing and including the world*. In the words of Ikhnaton, the ancient Egyptian pharaoh (ca. 1375–1358 B.C.) who worshiped the sun as the symbol of God:

Thou risest beautifully, O living Aton,
Lord of eternity;
Thy glowing hue brings life to the hearts of men,
When thou hast filled the two lands with thy love.
O God, who himself fashioned himself,
Maker of every land.[7]

Hartshorne and Reese maintain that there are five characteristics to the doctrine of panentheism: Panentheism, properly understood, means the belief that there is a God, who is (1) eternal in some respects; (2) temporal, that is, in some aspects capable of change; (3) conscious, or self-aware; (4) knowing the world or universe, or omniscient; and (5) world-inclusive, having all things as constituents of his fullness.[8]

Such a vision of God is said to be the essential theological position of Plato, Schelling, Fechner, Whitehead, and the Hindu thinker Radhakrishnan.[9]

An Immodest Proposal

Panentheism, to a large degree, is one of the most vital elements in the theological work of American theologians over the past few decades. It is hardly a new concept, as we can see from the names of the thinkers who have embraced its doctrine. If we accept other thinkers who have held most, but not all, of the five principles laid out by Hartshorne and Reese as panentheists, then we might add to the list William James, Ehressfels, and Brightman, and to a degree, the pantheists Spinoza and Royce. We would definitely have to admit Charles Hartshorne[10] as a panentheist, and Joseph Haroutunian[11] despite his orthodox language, as well as Schubert M. Ogden,[12] Ralph E. James,[13] and Thomas W. Ogletree.[14]

We would certainly have to recognize John B. Cobb,

Jr., William A. Christian, Daniel Day Williams, George L. Kline, Bernard Loomer, Donald W. Sherburne, and even the late French philosophical theologian Teilhard de Chardin,[15] as holding to pantheistic beliefs also.

The Unity of Nature and Spirit in a New Panentheism as the Possible Religion of the Future

I would like to suggest a possible way in which panentheism might be developed by an explicit unification with certain very strong emotional feelings that have recently developed from the side of the life sciences concerning man's responsibility to care for the whole earth, including but not limited to mankind. My suggestion is that the theological doctrines of panentheism might be logically united to the strong sense of mankind's obligation to care for the earth and to save it from the physical destruction man is now visiting upon it. What I am suggesting is the development of a theology of environmental awareness. This means that we can take the celebration of the first Earth Day in April, 1970, as a kind of Easter for the now unsystematized but nevertheless real theology of the earth that is growing among sensitive people all over America and abroad. I believe that such a development might bring forth a religion that could cover the needs that for so long have been unmet by the organized theology of the church and which have become increasingly evident in the rise of interest in the occult.

I believe that I am only following the kind of concerned religious teaching that Leslie D. Weatherhead has written about in his book *The Christian Agnostic*,[16] where he states:

I believe passionately that Christianity is a way of life, not a theological system with which one must be in intellectual agreement. I feel that Christ would admit into discipleship anyone who sincerely desired to follow him, and allow that disciple to make his creed out of this experience; to listen, to consider, to pray, to follow, and ultimately to believe only those convictions about which the experience of fellowship made him sure.[17]

Some Wild Guesses at the True Meaning of Reformation

What I am saying here is not so much the result of a study of history or an analysis of certain ideas as it is a kind of reaction to the evidently threadbare quality of so much that passes for Christian theology. I would like to raise the wild question of whether or not it is possible that each reformation of religion in the history of Western man has been the bringing into the "revealed" tradition (that is, Judaism, Christianity, and Islam) of a revitalizing shot of paganism. By paganism I mean a religion of nature, an inclusive religion of mankind in general, in distinction from that exclusive religion which taught the election of the peculiar people by God. This exclusive emphasis in the basic traditions of the West first expressed itself in the belief that God had called one tribe, the people of Israel, into a special relationship with himself, and that emphasis led to such pride that the prophets were needed to universalize the message. It is true that the religion of the Old Testament succeeded in making its faith a universal one, but the exclusiveness never left it either. Part of this exclusiveness expressed itself in the crystallizing of the Old Testament teaching into a book, so that Judaism became a religion of the word—indeed, of the written word.

Following the idea of inclusiveness as opposed to exclusiveness, we might see the prophets as introducers of a pagan element into religion by their stress on the rights of the Gentiles. They stressed equal justice for all and clearly taught that God demands mercy and not sacrifice. The prophet that we know as II Isaiah even referred to the pagan emperor Cyrus as a messiah or Christ (Isa. 45:1).

Although it is true that the few teachings that were recorded from the lips of Christ do not contain as many natural or pagan elements as we sometimes might wish (for example, with reference to sex), we must remember that only a minimum number of his words were selected for emphasis and retention. We do find, even in what the various church thinkers retain, a universal emphasis that stresses that God is the God of the Gentiles also and that if the Jews would not listen, Christ would abandon them and turn to the Gentiles. There are a number of Gospel passages that do show the earthiness and humanity of Jesus, however. Among these are the stories of Jesus' attendance at the wedding feast in Cana, and the charges of his enemies that he was a winebibber and the friend of gluttons. Finally, Jesus' parting command was for his disciples to go into all the world and not just to certain people.

The writings of Paul seem clearly to be a never-ending battle against an exclusive view of Christianity as tied to Judaism with its rites and ceremonies. Paul stressed that Christ had come for all and that his way was open and free to all regardless of background. Paul taught that the Gentiles needed no circumcision and that in the matter of salvation the Jew had no advantage over others. Without unduly stressing the accommodation of Christ's message to the Greek mentality in the teachings of Paul, we must still recognize that the terminology that he used was drawn from the common Greek pagan religious tradition.

In the case of the rise of Islam, Muhammad came stressing the universality of God and the availability of God's mercy and justice to all men. The only exclusiveness of the Islamic faith was the belief that all should reverence Allah, and Islam developed as one of the least racially biased social movements ever to appear in history.

Turning through the pages of history to the era of the Reformation, we come to Martin Luther, who perhaps more than anyone else brought traditional Christianity into touch with the developing culture of northern Europe. He stressed the personal freedom of man and the availability of and the necessity for the individual's own inner relationship with God. He founded his church on a territorial basis and reintroduced into Christianity a number of the pagan Germanic customs such as a sacred tree, now called the Christmas tree, while at the same time throwing out the older, more Mediterranean pagan elements that he found in medieval Roman Catholicism.

Friedrich Schleiermacher, beginning in 1799, began writing in the defense of what he thought was the real essence of religion[18] in order to show that it is not just the concern of the uncultured and old-fashioned people of the world but something that belongs to the truly cultured, fully developed human being, who without religion lacks the noblest element of life. Schleiermacher established the basis of religion in human feelings and made it clear that all men can be religious. In this way he universalized religion and made it a part of the natural order of things, making the gap between revealed religion and paganism almost nil. In this approach to faith, Schleiermacher, of course, is a forerunner of the development of human psychology as a discipline.

After the midpoint of the twentieth century, the writers Thomas Altizer, William Hamilton, and others brought forward the views which they called Christian atheism. As I have written elsewhere extensively about this movement, I will only mention it here.[19] We may say that Christian atheism represents one of the many attempts of sensitive men to find a new basis for their spiritual lives in modern times. Gustave H. Todrank has named this great wave of religious searching in our day *The Secular Search for a New Christ*.[20]

Occultism, which we have been studying in this book, represents but one of the waves in the storm-tossed sea that modern men are crossing in their quest for new symbols to help them see themselves and the world in a healthy and satisfying light. Unfortunately, so much of Christian atheism, the "death of God" theology, and the various ways of the occult has become, in Todrank's words, a theology without God, a Christology without Jesus, a Bible without authority, a church without clergy, a salvation without immortality, and a morality without immorality. Now, perhaps, we can do with a Christology of a more spiritual type, and we can certainly do with a Bible that is interpreted in a less authoritative way. A church without clergy and without buildings would not be a loss at all. However, a theology without God in the sense of some conception of the ultimate meaning of the universe is impossible. Even Altizer has his sacred void and the writer Ernest Hemingway in the depths of his feelings of meaninglessness found himself praying "Our

Nada who art in Nada," which means "our nothingness."

Even nothingness is something when it figures in a theology and is addressed in prayer, but nothingness surely does not contain the positive power, even on the psychological level, to keep us going in the world. Something more is needed, and indeed our experience of human life gives us something more than nothing—it gives us the experience of human love and fellowship, compassion and courage, and that nagging sense of guilt and even of boredom which in a negative way reminds us of man's possibility of transcendence. I believe that these positive factors are best summed up in the historic myth of the Christ. I believe that all that men are searching for in the occult can be found more clearly in the myth of Christ when it is joined, as it must be again, to reverence for the earth and for every living thing. Today those who are interested in helping man to find spiritual assistance should seize upon the current recognition of millions that we are destroying the earth and ourselves and must begin to reverse this process. A theology that embraces that recognition along with Christ could be the answer, it seems to me, to the nagging quest for transcendence that is seen in the search of those following the occult. Such a theology could bring the release that is needed by those who in their frustration are turning to self-destruction through drugs or to destruction of others through war abroad and through violence at home.

If we could connect the myth of the resurrection with the general belief today that mankind needs to work for the regeneration of the earth, we would lay the foundation for an appealing panentheism. The idea of the dead Christ who was laid in the earth, where he germinated like a seed that burst through the soil into newness of life, needs to be joined to the desire of millions to aggressively conserve nature and regenerate men. There is a general public feeling today that mankind in its selfishness and shortsightedness has put to death much in itself that is noble and most human. Scientists declare in the tones and words of the revivalistic evangelist that we have already killed much of the limited pool of life on the earth.

Mankind has had its Good Friday in its many wars and its despoliation of the environment; now it is ready for a resurrection through the pursuit of an aggressive program of peace and a reversal of the mistreatment of nature. A panentheism founded on the new sensitivity of men to the holiness and uniqueness of life and nature could combine within itself the best of the revealed and natural religious traditions. In its stress on the goodness of creation and its basis in the recognition of the incarnation of man's ultimate concern in this world, it could be profoundly Christian.

Man cannot live without God, but man also cannot live without the earth. If there was a time when religion had to fight the divinization of the earth in the baal cults, that time is long past. Until we see the earth as part of God, we will continue to use it as if it were a sewer. To the degree that there is a vague religious feeling behind the sentiments of the environmentalists today, we already have the psychological basis for this religious doctrine. Hopefully, the first Earth Day will not be the last, and it may turn out to be a worldwide celebration of a new Easter that could signalize the revival and regeneration of man as a spiritual being.

EPILOGUE

After considering everything discussed in this book, I
have drawn one major conclusion, that is, that there is
a connection between the abuse of drugs and the rise of
so much interest in the occult. This conclusion rests
upon investigation of the activities of young people, to
be sure, and does not reflect upon the interest in astrology
and palm-reading of many middle-aged people, which
has a long tradition. Because of the fact that interest in
the occult among young people and interest in the use of
drugs both rest upon a sense of alienation from society,
I would also conclude that the most alienated occult
groups are the fastest-growing. I have seen a good deal
of evidence that backs up this insight. No one who knows
college-aged young people can be unaware of the deeply
disturbed minds of so many of them. No one who has
such people's trust can be unaware of how great is the
number of people in their teens and twenties who are
estranged to one degree or another from the aims of
governmental policy and the goals of institutional religion. In many, alienation from parents, teachers, clergy,
and college administrators is complete. And this is by no
means a condition that clears up upon graduation from
college. The military is now full of young men with this
attitude, as are the ranks of business. These estranged

people find their only release, oftentimes, in pot parties, acid trips on weekends, and—increasingly—in more or less satanic meetings in which sexual experimentation passes into sadism and masochism, and drug intoxication passes into psychotic episodes.

Witchcraft is real. This is another conclusion that must be drawn from this survey. Witchcraft is the practice of the power of suggestion by a person or persons of an aggressive frame of mind upon other persons of a hysterical (or highly suggestive) disposition. We seem to have a very great number of highly suggestive young people today. They are prey to the suggestibility of other people who turn them on to drugs, to casual sex, and—of late— to weird occult practices.

I have seen the tremendous psychic damage being done to many young people by the irresponsible use of debilitating drugs. The little worlds of black-magic groups everywhere are surrounded by larger worlds of other young people affected by the hard core. These fringe people show signs of fearfulness approaching paranoia and definite character disorganization from the misuse of the drugs they take at the "parties" of black witches. Against this evil we need not so much the enforcement of more laws, but the cleansing and enlightening teachings of a revitalized religion that has the power to cast out demons by a positive example of love and faith.

It is always easy to condemn offenders against the traditional moral code and persons guilty of breaking the laws of the state. Of course, literally thousands, perhaps millions, of young adults from high school age through their thirties are technically guilty of violating the various state and federal drug laws. Some estimates, which I consider conservative, say there are ten million marijuana smokers in America. There must be many thousands who use much harsher substances in a futile attempt to find a better reality. I do not commend these people, but I also do not condemn them, since the alienation of character that possesses them also possesses the rest of us. Those on the other side of the law are different only in degree from the remainder of us, not in kind. And the alienation and frustration that now possesses us is not the creation of any one of us, but the very atmosphere of our society.[1]

What I am saying, I suppose, is that the church should be the kind of agency that could meet the needs of people. It is not—at least not for the majority of the young, the educated, and the sensitive in the population. The many examples of human failure we see all around us are but reflections of a larger cultural and institutional failure that must be reversed and corrected before we can really help individual cases.

There are signs that the church, at least in some of its institutional expressions, is more open to change and revitalization than is the state. Movements in the various denominations toward new codes of sexual morality, expressions of great concern over the need to terminate the Indochina war, and the use of the church's influence to press for more scientifically based drug laws are all good signs. But, as yet, there are only signs. And, unfortunately, the liberalizing tendencies are usually at the top of churches, while the most conservative and punitive ideas remain strong on the local level, continuing to alienate the sensitive, young and old. Only when compassion for one another, the sense that sharing and giving are more important than having and consuming, the ideas that underlie Judaism, Christianity, and Buddhism, are made real by our living them will the searching minds among us find a releasing power greater than drugs and the lure of the occult. The Age of Aquarius, in its conception, is a wholesome ideal, but without the demonstration of God's people of the peace and love men long for, the religion of Aquarius may become one of disappointment, frustration, violence, and self-hate. If we are to cast out the demons of anxiety, fear, and self-doubt; the devils of undisciplined sensuality and self-abuse; the specters of a world continually involved in competition and warfare; it can only be by the expulsive power of a new affection for the God of love. In the offering of this new affection, we had best not offer a peace that passes understanding but an understanding of what makes for peace. And, instead of a vague and rhetorical love of an invisible God, the church would do better to show a love for the man whom we can see, and who desperately needs it.

NOTES

Foreword

1. This statement was prepared for the use of my students at Eastern Kentucky University as well as for my auditors at the many lectures I have given on youthful interest in the occult, at such places as the Veterans Administration Regional Hospital in Lexington, Kentucky, the University of Kentucky, and other college and professional psychological groups.

Introduction

1. Samuel J. Beck, "Four Searches for God in Man," *The University of Chicago Magazine,* Vol. LXII, No. 5 (March/April, 1970), p. 13.

Chapter I. The Occult in America Today

1. This "computerized horoscope" is from the Time Pattern Research Institute, Inc., Valley Stream, N.Y. It costs $20. Other computerized horoscopes are available, including "Astroprofile," sold by mail by The Universe Book Club, Garden City, N.Y., for $10.

2. See *TV Guide,* October 4–10, 1969, pp. 6–8; *Time,* March 21, 1969, pp. 47–56; and *Hair,* by Gerome Ragni and James Rado (Pocket Books, 1969). Also see *Philadelphia* magazine, January, 1970, pp. 49–54, and the entire March 1970 issue of *McCall's.*

3. See John C. Cooper, *The New Mentality* (The Westminster Press, 1969).

4. W. B. Yeats, "The Second Coming," from *The Golden Treasury,* ed. by Oscar Williams (Mentor Books, New American Library, Inc., 1959).

5. See Bishop James A. Pike, with Diane Kennedy, *The Other Side* (Dell Publishing Company, Inc., 1969).

6. Martin Heidegger, *Being and Time,* tr. by John Macquarrie and Edward Robinson (Harper & Row, Publishers, Inc., 1962), pp. 69 and *passim.*

7. In connection with the discussion of the hippie movement among the young and the rise of "cults of evil," see my *The New Mentality; The Killing of Sharon Tate,* told by Susan Atkins to Lawrence Schiller (Signet Books, New American Library, Inc., 1970); and *Esquire,* Vol. LXXIII, No. 3 (March, 1970), pp. 99 ff. Also see "Love Among the Rattlesnakes," by Jean Stafford, in *McCall's,* March, 1970, pp. 69, 145–146.

8. John C. Cooper, *The Turn Right* (The Westminster Press, 1970).

9. See *Vajra Bodhi Sea,* a magazine published for The Orthodox Buddhadharma in America, by the Sino-American Buddhist Association, 125 Waverly Place, San Francisco, Calif. 94108.

10. Alfred North Whitehead, *Science in the Modern World* (Mentor Books, New American Library, Inc., 1964), p. 171.

11. Julio Caro Baroja, *The World of the Witches,* tr. by O. N. V. Glendinning (The University of Chicago Press, 1964).

12. *Ibid.,* pp. XII–XIII.

13. See Erik H. Erikson, *Childhood and Society* (W. W. Norton & Company, Inc., 1963).

14. The materials presented here that discuss the generation gap are drawn from the author's series of articles

entitled "The New Mentality," in *Insight*, Vol. 2, Nos. 6–8 (February/March, 1970), published by the Board of Parish Education, Lutheran Church in America, 2900 Queen Lane, Philadelphia, Pa. 19129.

15. Erik H. Erikson, *Insight and Responsibility* (W. W. Norton & Company, 1964), pp. 88–89.

16. *Ibid.*, p. 90.

17. Harvey Cox, quoted in "A Conversation with Harvey Cox and T. George Harris," *Psychology Today*, Vol. 3, No. 11 (April, 1970), p. 45.

Chapter II. COMICS, MOVIES, MEDIUMS, AND MURDER

1. Harvey Cox, quoted in "A Conversation with Harvey Cox and T. George Harris," *loc. cit.*, p. 45.

2. *Ibid.*, p. 47.

3. *Ibid.*, p. 62.

4. William Hamilton, in *Celluloid and Symbols*, ed. by John C. Cooper and Carl Skrade (Fortress Press, 1970), p. 72.

5. *Ibid.*

6. See Ch. I, note 5, above.

7. Pike, *op. cit.*, p. 229.

8. *Ibid.*, p. 32.

9. Marie Louise von Franz, "C. G. Jung and the Problems of Our Time," *Quadrant*, No. 5 (Fall, 1969), p. 6.

10. Curt Gentry, *The Late, Great State of California* (G. P. Putnam's Sons, 1968).

11. See James Kallas, *Jesus and the Power of Satan* (The Westminster Press, 1968), and his *The Satanward View* (The Westminster Press, 1966).

12. John Milton, *Paradise Lost*, Book IV, lines 75–111.

13. Tom Burke, "Princess Leda's Castle in the Air," *Esquire*, Vol. LXXIII, No. 3 (March, 1970), p. 104.

14. See Pennethorne Hughes, *Witchcraft* (Pelican Books, Penguin Books, Inc., 1965); Gerald B. Gardner,

Witchcraft Today (Arrow Books, 1966); and Sir Walter Scott, *Letters on Demonology and Witchcraft* (Ace Books, 1970).

15. Arthur Miller, *The Crucible*, in *Best Plays of 1952–53*, ed. by Louis Kronenberger (Dodd, Mead & Company, Inc., 1953).

16. See Sybil Leek, *Diary of a Witch* (Signet Books, New American Library, Inc., 1968).

17. Robert Darnton, *Mesmerism and the End of the Enlightenment in France* (Harvard University Press, 1968).

18. See Anton Szandor LaVey, *The Satanic Bible* (Avon Books, 1969), and Judith Rascoe, "Church of Satan," *McCall's*, March, 1970, pp. 75 ff.

Chapter III. NEW MEANINGS IN THE SYMBOLS OF THE OCCULT

1. See Baroja, *op. cit.*

2. *Ibid.*, p. 14.

3. *Ibid.*, p. 32.

4. Information from *National Geographic*, Vol. 137, No. 4 (April, 1970), pp. 536–539.

5. E. F. Edinger, "Alchemy as a Psychological Process," *Quadrant*, No. 2 (Fall, 1968).

6. *Ibid.*

7. On shamans, the best authority to consult is Mircea Eliade. See Mircea Eliade: *Cosmos and History* (Harper Torchbooks, 1959), *The Sacred and the Profane* (Harper Torchbooks, 1961), *Patterns in Comparative Religion* (Meridian Books, New American Library, Inc., 1963), *Rites and Symbols of Initiation* (Harper Torchbooks, 1965), *Myths, Dreams, and Mysteries* (Harper Torchbooks, 1967).

8. *The Alan Watts Journal*, March, 1970, p. 3.

9. Stephen Lovett, "The Cultivating Scholar," *Vajra Bodhi Sea,* Vol. I, No. 1 (April, 1970), pp. 28–29.

10. *The Alan Watts Journal,* March, 1970, p. 3.

11. Heng Ch'ien, in *Vajra Bodhi Sea,* Vol. I, No. 1 (April, 1970), p. 19.

12. *The Alan Watts Journal,* March, 1970, p. 4.

13. Rudolf Otto, *The Idea of the Holy* (Oxford University Press, Inc., 1936).

14. See my *The New Mentality.*

15. Arthur C. Clarke, *2001: A Space Odyssey* (New American Library, Inc., 1968).

16. John C. Cooper, *The Roots of the Radical Theology* (The Westminster Press, 1967).

17. John C. Cooper, *Radical Christianity and Its Sources* (The Westminster Press, 1968).

18. Marshall McLuhan and Quentin Fiore, *War and Peace in the Global Village* (Bantam Books, Inc., 1968).

19. Vittorio Lanternari, *The Religions of the Oppressed* (Mentor Books, New American Library, Inc., 1965).

20. Robert A. Heinlein's now-famous science fantasy, *Stranger in a Strange Land,* speaks to the younger generation and to us specifically because it offers us an alternative future that is like and yet unlike life in the present. Not even the fact that the science fiction in this novel, first published in 1961, has been overtaken by science fact makes it untenable for us. Heinlein begins his famous novel by saying that it takes 258 days to travel from Mars to Earth. Actually, the science of missiles and space travel has caught up with that projection of technology. But the idea of a person who is human but not quite human, Valentine Michael Smith, coming into our culture and seeing some of the trivial things that exercise us, has not been and cannot be outflanked by scientific development. Valentine Smith speaks to the disturbed, the alienated,

and the concerned among our young people, as well as to the sick (for example, Charles Manson), for Valentine clearly articulates what they too feel is wrong with our society.

The following quotation from an actual letter written by an American student in Canada to the author ought to make clear the nonresponsiveness and ineffectiveness of so much of American literature today: "I saw the funeral of Martin Luther King, Jr., today and was deeply moved by both his death and our plight. Our country's cart seems hitched to the horses of galloping insanity and now perhaps the strongest reasonable voice is gone . . . but perhaps also now that he is 'immortalized,' as charismatic people tend to be, his past voice will be even more powerful. I hope so—I cannot imagine what will happen if we who know don't do something and if those in power don't find out. I'm sick of poverty programs and of neighborhood street-sweeping campaigns; they're all wonderful and pretty effective underneath all the red tape but we need a massive plan, an economic strategy, a way to put the pressure on business and homeowners so that the black man in America can walk economically, geographically, and politically free . . . , not worry about being loved after all this, since if we are to wait for the hearts of people we will wait forever. The answer is not easy but I think it is clear. In the meantime, what do we do? One compelling reason that I want to return to New York is to do something, but the more I think about it the smaller whatever I'll do appears."

The field of science fiction, on its science fantasy side, is already in touch with the rising area of interest in the occult. For years many "books" and stories (most, to be sure, of poor literary quality) have been produced and bought by a growing market for escape literature. For some years *The Magazine of Fantasy and Science Fiction* has presented both new stories by men such as Isaac Asimov and articles about classic writers such as H. P. Love-craft. In 1966, *F. and S. F.* had a paid circulation of 60,000 and it produced French, German, Italian, Spanish, and Japanese editions. Additionally, there are magazines called *Analog—Astounding Science Fiction* and *Venture Science Fiction.* Paperback Library, Inc., of New York, publishes several series of books by authors such as Jane Gaskell, including her *The City* (about Cija, a princess of Atlantis), *Atlan,* and *The Serpent.* Harcourt, Brace and World, Inc., of New York, publishes such books as *Operation Time Search,* by Andre Norton, which re-counts a war between Atlantis and the equally lost con-tinent of Mu. By 1967, Norton had already produced thirty books in this genre, including *Witch World, Web of the Witch World,* and *Three Against the Witch World,* as well as others. We can easily see the close connection between the occult and interest in science fiction just by a study of these titles. However, it is probably in the more "usual" area of science fiction that we find both a consist-ent attempt to give men a series of alternative futures and a critique of current moral and social ills.

Chapter IV. POLITICS AND AQUARIUS

1. Norman Mailer, *The Armies of the Night* (New American Library, Inc., 1968).

2. See *The National Observer,* May 25, 1970. James M. Perry reported on the supposedly "calm" and "con-servative" campus of Eastern Kentucky University, find-ing it still calm, but not as conservative as it once was, in his article "Kevin Phillip's 'Calm' Campus Also Proves to Be Agitated."

3. The quotations are from Daniel Frilling, philoso-phy major, Eastern Kentucky University, 1970, and Deb-orah Hunefeldt, German major, E.K.U., 1972. Used by permission.

4. See *The Southern Journal of Philosophy,* Vol. VIII, No. 2 (Summer, 1970), with R. Baine Harris acting as guest editor, for a complete reporting of the papers read at the 1968 conference on "Philosophers and the Crisis of Authority" held at Clemson University. The author presented a paper at the conference on the theme "The Crisis of Authority in the Protestant Churches of the United States."

5. Kenneth L. Woodward, "Séances in Suburbia," *McCall's,* March, 1970, p. 149.

6. Milton Himmelfarb, *Commentary,* Vol. 49, No. 4 (April, 1970), p. 41.

7. See Donald Nugent, "The City of God Revisited," *Cross Currents,* Summer, 1969.

8. *The Satires of Juvenal,* tr. by Herbert Creekmore (Mentor Books, New American Library, Inc, 1963).

9. *Ibid.,* p. 31; lines 115–116.

10. Aldous Huxley, *Brave New World* (Bantam Books, Inc., 1958).

11. George Orwell, *1984* (Harcourt, Brace and World, Inc., 1949.

12. Ray Bradbury, *Fahrenheit 451* (Ballantine Books, Inc., 1953).

13. Ronald Reichers, physics major, E.K.U., 1970. Used by permission.

14. Thomas Cayton, physics major, E.K.U., 1970. Used by permission.

15. Anatole France, *Penguin Island* (Bantam Books, Inc., 1958).

16. Anthony Standen, *Science Is a Sacred Cow* (E. P. Dutton & Company, Inc., 1950) .

17. Aldous Huxley, *Brave New World Revisited* (Bantam Books, Inc., 1960).

18. Robert A. Heinlein, *Stranger in a Strange Land* (Avon Books, 1966). See Ch. III, note 20, above.

19. J. R. R. Tolkien, *The Lord of the Rings* (Ballantine Books, 1965).

Chapter V. SEX, DRUGS, EMPIRICISM, AND MYSTICISM

1. Max Metcalf, "Drug Addiction," *Lutheran Social Welfare*, Spring, 1970, p. 6.

2. Phyllis Browning, Eastern Kentucky University, Nursing, 1970. Used by permission.

3. Donald Nugent, "The Future of Witchcraft," unpublished manuscript presented to *Logos*, The Philosophy Club of Eastern Kentucky University, May 14, 1970.

4. Chadwick Hansen, *Witchcraft at Salem* (Signet Books, New American Library, Inc., 1969).

5. *Ibid.*, pp. IX–X.

6. Letter to the author from Donald Nugent, May 25, 1970.

7. Hansen, *op. cit.*, pp. 31–32.

8. The information on the "voodoo death" syndrome is from Dr. Kenneth Kuhn, Captain, Medical Corps, U.S. Army, Blue Grass Army Ordinance Depot, Richmond, Ky.

9. See Sajon's *Analytic Cyclopedia of Practical Medicine* (7th ed., Philadelphia: F. A. Davis Co., 1917), Vol. II, pp. 1–11, or any comparable medical encyclopedia.

10. Hansen, *op. cit.*, p. 39.

11. Article in the Richmond, Ky., *Daily Register*, May 27, 1970.

12. Nugent, "The City of God Revisited," *loc. cit.*

13. Norman Mailer, in *Harpers Magazine*, March, 1968, p. 83.

14. John Updike, *Couples* (Alfred A. Knopf, Inc., 1968).

15. Brooks R. Walker, *The New Immorality* (Doubleday & Company, Inc., 1968).

16. Nugent, "The Future of Witchcraft," *loc. cit.*

17. Hughes, *op. cit.* See Ch. II, note 14.

18. Gardner, *op. cit.* See Ch. II, note 14.

19. See Vatsyayana, *The Kama Sutra: The Hindu Ritual of Love* (Castle Books, 1963).

20. Alan Watts, *This Is It, And Other Essays on Zen and Spiritual Experience* (Pantheon Books, Inc., 1960).

21. Daniel L. Frilling, E.K.U. philosophy major, 1970. The quotation is from a paper, "The Philosophy of Henri Bergson and the World of the Living." Used by permission.

22. Metcalf, "Drug Addiction," *loc. cit.,* p. 10.

23. *Ibid.,* p. 9.

Chapter VI. EXTRAPOLATIONS ON THE FUTURE

1. MDA is the name for *meta diox. amphetamine,* a variety of the amphetamine group, known as "meth" or "speed" by drug users. See *The Journal of the American Medical Association,* February 2, 1970.

2. Paul Tillich, *Systematic Theology* (The University of Chicago Press, 1963), Vol. III, pp. 152, 153, 154, 169, 181, 182, 220, 246, 247, 366, 376, 379, and 382.

3. Daniel L. Frilling, "The Yang and Yin of Life," unpublished manuscript. Used by permission.

4. *Ibid.*

5. Josiah Royce, *The Religious Aspect of Philosophy* (Houghton Mifflin Company, 1885), Ch. 12.

6. Charles Hartshorne and William L. Reese (eds.), *Philosophers Speak of God* (The University of Chicago Press, 1963).

7. *Ibid.,* p. 29. Italics mine.

8. *Ibid.,* p. 16.

9. *Ibid.,* p. 17.

10. See Charles Hartshorne, *The Divine Relativity* (Yale University Press, 1964).

11. See Joseph Haroutunian, *God with Us: A Theology of Transpersonal Life* (The Westminster Press, 1965).

12. See Schubert M. Ogden, *The Reality of God and Other Essays* (Harper & Row, Publishers, Inc., 1966).

13. See Ralph E. James, *The Concrete God* (The Bobbs-Merrill Company, Inc., 1967).

14. See Thomas W. Ogletree, *The Death of God Controversy* (Abingdon Press, 1966).

15. See Teilhard de Chardin: *The Phenomenon of Man* (Harper Torchbooks, 1961), *The Future of Man* (Harper & Row, Publishers, Inc., 1964), *The Divine Milieu* (Harper Torchbooks, 1965), and *The Vision of the Past* (Harper & Row, Publishers, Inc., 1966).

16. Leslie D. Weatherhead, *The Christian Agnostic* (Abingdon Press, 1965).

17. *Ibid.*, p. 16.

18. See Friedrich Schleiermacher, *On Religion: Speeches to Its Cultured Despisers* (Harper Torchbooks, 1958).

19. See my *The Roots of the Radical Theology* and *Radical Christianity and Its Sources.*

20. Gustave H. Todrank, *The Secular Search for a New Christ* (The Westminster Press, 1969).

EPILOGUE

1. See Rosa Gustaitis, *Turning On* (Signet Books, New American Library, Inc., 1970), for an excellent account of the part drugs play in the "turned on" generation.

DATE DUE
